The International
Student's Survival Guide

The International Student's Survival Guide

How to get the most from studying at a UK university

Gareth Davey

Los Angeles • London • New Delhi • Singapore

First published 2008

Apart from any fair dealing for the purposes of research or
private study, or criticism or review, as permitted under the Copyright, Designs
and Patents Act, 1988, this publication
may be reproduced, stored or transmitted in any form, or
by any means, only with the prior permission in writing of
the publishers, or in the case of reprographic reproduction, in
accordance with the terms of licences issued by the Copyright
Licensing Agency. Enquiries concerning reproduction outside those terms
should be sent to the publishers.

SAGE Publications Ltd
1 Oliver's Yard
55 City Road
London EC1Y 1SP

SAGE Publications Inc.
2455 Teller Road
Thousand Oaks, California 91320

SAGE Publications India Pvt Ltd
B 1/I 1 Mohan Cooperative Industrial Area
Mathura Road, Post Bag 7
New Delhi 110 044

SAGE Publications Asia-Pacific Pte Ltd
33 Pekin Street #02-01
Far East Square
Singapore 048763

Library of Congress Control Number 2007932290

British Library Cataloguing in Publication data

A catalogue record for this book is available
from the British Library

ISBN 978-1-4129-4601-8
ISBN 978-1-4129-4602-5 (pbk)

Typeset by C&M Digitals (P) Ltd, Chennai, India
Printed in Great Britain by The Cromwell Press Ltd, Trowbridge, Wiltshire
Printed on paper from sustainable resources

Contents

Introduction

This guide provides valuable advice for international students who are interested in studying at university in the UK. It gives all the information you need to make a suitable choice about where to study, and how to settle into your new surroundings.

Studying in the UK has many benefits. British universities are world-renowned and have excellent teaching and research standards. You will also be able to experience and enjoy the country's customs, culture, and daily life. Further, studying in an English-speaking country, surrounded by native speakers, will help you to improve your English language and communication skills. After you finish your course, you will have the qualifications, experience, and skills to excel in your career.

Studying in another country is a big step and should be considered carefully. The education system, customs, and social life will be unfamiliar, and you will need to learn to acclimatise to them. This book helps you along every step of the journey: from preparing to leave your country, through to the options available after graduation. There are ten self-contained units that cover a different stage of student life:

- Choosing and applying for your course
- Leaving home and arriving in the UK
- English language requirements
- Living costs and tuition fees
- Daily life and culture in the UK
- Health, welfare and safety
- Academic culture
- Teaching and assessment methods
- Study skills for academic success
- Life after graduation.

Every chapter is packed with information to make your stay in the UK more enjoyable. Throughout this guide there are checklists and self-evaluation forms to assess your skills and to keep on top of what needs to be done. The final section – a glossary and contacts directory – enables you to understand and find out more about the topics covered.

Overall, this guide will help you to succeed in your studies and will ensure that your time as a student will be fun and memorable. Studying in the UK will be one of the most exciting and challenging periods of your life. Enjoy it!

Gareth Davey

1 Choosing and applying for your course

INTRODUCTION

After reading this chapter, you should be able to:

- ☑ Recognise the benefits of studying in the UK
- ☑ Identify different types of courses
- ☑ Judge the suitability of courses
- ☑ Understand the application process
- ☑ Apply for a course

There are over 300 universities and colleges in the UK, offering thousands of higher education courses. Which one should you choose? To make your decision easier, this chapter provides information about the types of qualifications available, the factors to consider when choosing a course and university, and how to apply.

Why should I study in the UK?

There are many benefits of studying and living in the UK. The education system has an excellent reputation, and it is internationally recognised. The quality of teaching and learning is high. Further, courses focus on the development of skills, as well as subject knowledge, which will enable you to learn valuable attributes such as problem solving, critical and creative thinking, independence, and group work. These skills will aid your personal development and success after graduation. Studying in the UK will also allow you to experience its rich culture, improve your English skills, and access other European countries during your vacations.

Types of courses

A wide range of undergraduate (first degree) and postgraduate courses are available. Most undergraduate programmes lead to a Bachelor's degree. Students who do not have appropriate entry requirements for a degree might be able to start with a lower level qualification such as a Higher National Diploma or Foundation Degree. The majority of university programmes fall under the following classifications.

Certificate in Higher Education   This programme is one year (full-time) in duration. It covers the underlying concepts of a subject and develops skills such as problem solving. It is generally equivalent to the first year of an undergraduate degree.

Higher National Diploma and Foundation Degree   These courses are work-related and involve more detailed study and application of topics. Foundation degrees are designed and taught in partnership with employers to provide job-related knowledge and skills. They are equivalent to the first two years of an undergraduate degree. If completed successfully, they can lead to entry on to the third year of a Bachelor degree.

Bachelor degree   This is an undergraduate degree that covers advanced knowledge and application of study skills and takes three or four years to complete (subjects such as medicine and dentistry require longer). Traditionally, degrees are awarded with or without Honours (Honours is regarded as a higher level); if a student does not achieve the Honours standard, they may be awarded an Ordinary degree (see Chapter 8).

Benefits of studying in the UK?

Studying in the UK has many benefits:

- *Internationally recognized and respected qualifications*. The UK higher education system is world-renowned. A degree or other qualification will demonstrate your knowledge and skills, and will enhance your career prospects.
- *Quality*. Universities have excellent teaching and learning standards. Academic quality is checked regularly to ensure good quality teaching and learning experiences.
- *Accessibility and variety*. There is a range of access routes to higher education, and attendance on many courses is flexible. There is also a wide variety of programmes.
- *Shorter and intensive degrees save time and money*. Some courses, particularly three-year undergraduate degrees and one-year Master degrees, are shorter in duration compared to equivalent courses in other countries.
- *Research excellence*. UK universities have excellent research profiles and facilities.
- *British culture and easy access to Europe*. The UK has a rich culture and history that can be explored during your leisure time. It is also easy and inexpensive to travel to other European countries during your vacations.
- *Immersion in an English language environment*. Studying in an English-speaking country, surrounded by native speakers, will help you to improve your English language and communication skills.

- *Personal development.* Courses will develop your skills and personal qualities. Experience in another country and culture will also widen your perspective on life.
- *Emigration.* It may be possible to stay in the UK after graduation, for further study or for other reasons.
- *Fun! Life is all about having fun, and enjoying yourself.* There are many opportunities to enjoy an active social life.

Some universities offer courses that lead only to ordinary degrees with the option, possibly, to achieve the 'Honours' level as an add-on. However, nowadays most degrees are Honours degrees. Courses either cover a single subject (called 'single Honours'), equal coverage of two subjects (joint Honours), or an unequal combination of two (combined Honours).

Graduate Certificate and Diploma   These are postgraduate courses (a higher level than a bachelor degree). They involve advanced knowledge and development of study skills. A postgraduate course can also serve as a conversion course to introduce a new subject. A popular course is the Post Graduate Certificate in Education (PGCE), which is a teaching qualification that prepares graduates for teaching in schools, as well as in colleges and universities.

Master degree   A Master degree is a postgraduate programme that teaches advanced knowledge and analysis of complex issues. It enables a high development of study skills, particularly research skills. Master degrees can be either taught courses, research-based, or a combination of both. They are one or two years in duration. A popular Master degree is the MBA (Master of Business Administration), which covers management and business skills. Some Master degrees, such as arts degrees in Scotland, and Integrated Master programmes in engineering, science, and mathematics, are actually four-year undergraduate programmes that include postgraduate study.

Doctorate   A range of doctorate degrees are available. A PhD is a doctoral research degree that involves a detailed investigation and evaluation of a topic and leads to the creation of new knowledge. It involves advanced research techniques and academic enquiry. Other courses, particularly professional doctorates, have a substantial taught part and emphasise professional practice more than academic scholarship. A new type of PhD is the 'New Route PhD', which is interdisciplinary, and includes taught courses alongside the development of professional skills and a research project.

There are other types of courses available in UK universities. They include:

- Diploma in health (a three-year course in health-related areas such as midwifery and nursing).
- Short courses that do not count towards a formal award.

- Access routes (e.g., Foundation Programmes) for students without appropriate entry requirements for a bachelor degree.
- A period of study in the UK that forms part of qualification awarded by a university in another country (e.g., study abroad schemes). The most common type of arrangement is the Socrates-Erasmus programme, which enables students in European countries to study in the UK for part of their degree.
- An English language course.
- Distance learning and external degrees that are studied at home, away from a university.

The Socrates-Erasmus programme

The Socrates-Erasmus programme is a scheme that allows European students to study in the UK (or in another European country). Eligible students can study in the UK for a minimum of 3 months and a maximum of 12 months. The places and courses available depend on the arrangement between your university and their partner universities in the UK. Erasmus students do not pay tuition fees to the UK university and may be eligible for a grant towards expenses. Bear in mind, however, that courses in the UK require a high English language ability. Also, the cost of living can be higher than in some other European countries. Further details about the programme are available from the Socrates-Erasmus Council.

Choosing your course and university

Where should you study? Choosing the right place requires careful consideration and should not be a last-minute decision.

There is no 'best' university or course. Your choice will depend on your personal preference and the good and bad points of different options. Below is a list of factors to consider, including the characteristics of different universities and their courses, as well as your suitability. Use the information to help judge your options.

Your suitability

Think about the subjects that you enjoy and are good at. You are likely to get the best out of your studies by pursuing a course that you are keen on. If you are already in the UK, you can attend Open Days and Taster Courses offered by universities to learn more about the area you want to study and to check out a university's facilities. Also, think about your career aspirations and how they relate to different courses. For example, careers such as medicine and dentistry require the completion of specific courses, whereas other jobs are open to graduates who have studied in different disciplines.

Course characteristics

There are many differences between courses. Even courses with the same name can vary between universities! Things to think about include:

- entry requirements (including English language requirements)
- course length, syllabus, and modes of study
- career prospects
- teaching and assessment methods
- work placements and training opportunities included in the course
- credit transfer. If you have already completed an undergraduate course, you might be able to transfer credits to another course
- tuition fees and financial arrangements
- vocational courses tailored towards specific jobs, or academic ones that are not necessarily linked to any specific job or career
- courses can be accredited or approved by professional organisations, and offer partial exemption from professional qualifications: examples include accounting courses, marketing management (Chartered Institute of Marketing), psychology degrees (British Psychological Society), and journalism (National Council for the Training of Journalists)
- recognition of the course in your country
- courses designed specifically for international students.

Course details are available from university prospectuses and websites, and higher education fairs and Open Days.

Entry requirements

Most courses have entry requirements, such as qualifications, exam scores, English language ability, work experience and, in some cases, financial and medical conditions. Be realistic about how your qualifications and skills match the requirements of the courses you are interested in.

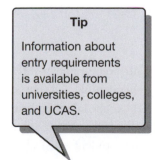

Tip

Information about entry requirements is available from universities, colleges, and UCAS.

Entry requirements can differ widely between courses and universities. The standard requirements for bachelor degrees are two or three GCE A-levels with GCSEs (in England, Wales, and Northern Ireland) or four or five Advanced Higher passes (in Scotland).

Requirements are described in terms of UK qualifications, so you will need to compare them with qualifications from your country. Advice is available from the Admissions Office at the universities you intend to study at. Further information is also available from the National Academic Recognition Information Centre (NARIC).

You should also check that the standard of your English is good enough (see Chapter 3). A few universities may require applicants to sit an admissions test, especially for courses in dental, law, medical and veterinary schools.

Reputation

Another factor to consider when choosing a university and course is their reputation with regards to the quality of teaching, research, and student support. There is no official list of universities based on their performance. However, national newspapers have produced unofficial league tables which indicate that certain universities and courses have higher quality than others. League tables can be accessed from the following guides:

- The *Times* Good University Guide
- The *Sunday Times* University Guide
- The *Guardian* University Guide
- The *Daily Telegraph* University league table
- The *Financial Times* League Table

Entry requirements differ between courses and universities. Table 1.1 lists in them as a general guide. All courses require proficiency in English (see Chapter 3).

League tables rank universities, and sometimes individual subjects, according to different performance criteria. The criteria include teaching and research quality, drop out rates, student satisfaction, staff-to-student ratio, library and computing facilities, and graduate employment rates. Each league table uses a different method to assess quality and, therefore, a university can have a different ranking on each table.

The league tables can be accessed via the websites directory at the end of this guide. You can use them to compare the performance of different universities; those at the top

Table 1.1   Entry requirements for courses in the UK

Type of course	Entry requirements	Duration
Certificate in Higher Education	Various. May require high school qualifications (e.g., GCE A-levels and GCSEs, or their equivalents), or no formal requirements.	One year (full-time)
Higher National Diploma; or Foundation degree	As above	Two years (full-time)
Foundation programme	As above	Six months or one year
Bachelor degree	High school qualifications	Three to four years full-time. Some courses, such as medicine and dentistry, require longer
Sandwich course (Bachelor degree)	Same as a Bachelor degree	Four or five years
Postgraduate Certificate; Postgraduate Diploma	Bachelor degree	The Certificate takes 9 months; the Diploma requires 10 months (full time)
Postgraduate Certificate of Education	Bachelor degree or Master degree	One year full-time
Master degree	Bachelor degree	Usually one year. Integrated Master programmes require four-years
PhD/DPhil	Bachelor degree (usually a 2.i), or a Master degree	Usually three or four years full-time
Professional Doctorate	Bachelor degree or a Master degree. May require professional qualifications and work experience	Two to four years full-time

are perceived as achieving a higher performance. Oxford and Cambridge tend to head the lists, followed usually by Imperial College and the London School of Economics (LSE). Other universities that often appear in the top ten are King's College London, University College London, University of Warwick and the University of York.

A few universities are traditionally distinguished in certain subjects, such as LSE for economics, and Imperial College for physics. The 'new universities' (those established in the 1960s, and previously known as polytechnics or colleges of higher education) occupy the lower sections of the tables. This is because they have traditionally focused on teaching technical and practical courses, whereas older universities placed more emphasis on research. However, the division between the two groups, and their position on league tables, has become blurred, as certain new universities now outperform older ones.

League tables are important because they are an indicator of quality. Some employers prefer graduates from top universities. News reports, for example, have claimed that graduates from high-ranking institutions earn higher salaries. Top universities are likely to have better research reputations and facilities, whereas universities lower on the list lead the latest developments in vocational courses.

However, your decision should not be based solely on league tables. They should be used as a general guide. Tables have been criticised because they do not include all measures of performance, do not include all universities, and are several years old. Choosing a university is a very personal decision, based on a variety of factors. The tables are useful, however, for providing information about the workings of universities and courses that interest you. If you do decide to use league tables, it is important to understand their good and bad points, and how their ratings are calculated; details are available from their websites.

Teaching and research quality

Every university has strict procedures to monitor and improve their quality. The law also regulates their power to award degrees. This assurance has led to good quality and the international reputation of British universities. However, academic quality varies between universities and departments. You can consider teaching and research quality when you choose somewhere to study. Data is available from two independent organisations that regularly assess the academic quality of universities:

- *Quality Assurance Agency* (QQA). Visits every university department and inspects their quality of teaching, support, assessment and learning opportunities.
- *Research Assessment Exercise* (RAE). Assesses research quality conducted every 4–5 years.

Results are available from their websites. However, the quality assessments should be considered with caution; they are not league tables and every university has strengths and weaknesses. Another way to gauge the quality of a university, if you are already in the UK, is to visit the university department that offers you a course and ask former students about their experiences there. Student feedback is also available from

- The Teaching Quality Information survey
- *Times* Higher Student Satisfaction Rating.

Oxbridge

Oxford and Cambridge universities are collectively known as 'Oxbridge'. They are the oldest and most famous universities in the UK, and have a reputation for academic excellence. Many famous politicians, scientists and other distinguished people have studied at them. Oxford and Cambridge have a number of well known traditions; for example, the two universities compete with each other at an annual Boat Race, which dates back to 1829.

Oxford and Cambridge have a collegiate structure. This means that each university consists of more than 30 colleges and every student is a member of a college and their university. This system enables students to belong to both a large university and to enjoy a smaller college community. The college is the focus of academic and social life (where students live and study), whereas the university is primarily responsible for teaching, exams, and awarding degrees.

If you want to apply to Oxford or Cambridge, you should bear in mind that there is intense competition for places; an excellent academic background and references are required. The application process starts earlier than most other universities, and there are earlier closing dates. For undergraduate applications, you must complete a university application form in addition to the UCAS form. There are differences in the application process for students in different countries, so you should read up-to-date information from each university's prospectus and website.

Career prospects and employability of recent graduates

It is worth looking at the employment record and destinations of recent graduates at specific universities, courses, and for the UK overall. The data could provide insights about your future career prospects. Information is available from:

- universities and their departments
- a university's career's centre
- the Higher Education Statistics Agency. They produce a report titled 'Destination of leavers from Higher Education'
- the Prospects website.

Location, size and safety

Universities differ in their type, size, location and surroundings. Think about the type of place you would prefer to live and study in.

Undergraduate and postgraduate courses can be studied at universities, university colleges, or colleges/institutes of higher education. Some courses, such as HNDs and Foundation degrees, are also available at Colleges of Further Education, which mainly cater for education up to the age of 18 and provide lower level courses for school leavers.

Location should also be considered. Universities are based in towns and cities, or in rural locations. Urban universities may be in the city centre, or in a suburb and areas vary in their pleasantness and safety. Rural universities have many amenities on campus but may be cut off from the outside world. Consider the availability of services such as banks, shops, supermarkets, and whether they are in walking distance to your lodgings. It is worthwhile to consider local transport services, and whether the university has restrictions on student parking (which could determine whether or not you can drive to your lectures if you intend to own a car).

Large universities can have more than 30,000 students, whereas smaller colleges have less than 1,000. Smaller institutions are likely to have smaller class sizes and, therefore, more interaction between students and professors, and a strong sense of community. However, larger universities will have a wide variety of courses, an established research reputation, good facilities, and ample social and entertainment facilities.

Another point to bear in mind is the diversity of the student population. Universities differ in their mix of international students, mature students, etc.

Facilities, support, and social life

Good universities provide excellent facilities and support services such as libraries, computer and internet access, laboratories, teaching equipment, and sporting facilities.

There should also be health and welfare services, such as university medical and dental care, childcare for students with children, counselling, and places of religious worship (see Chapter 6). If you have a disability, it is important to find out the type of support available, how much it costs, and, if applicable, whether buildings can be accessed (see Chapter 6).

> **Tip**
>
> If you are in the UK, you can attend an Open Day to tour the university and academic departments, and ask students about their experiences.

Some universities have a large and active Student Union that has a bar and organises social events. They could have student groups and societies about social, political and academic issues, which are good places to meet new friends, socialise, and pursue your interests.

Support for international students

Look for a university that has a good support system for students from outside the UK, including specialist advice and help for studying and settling in. Support services typically include:

- international student advisors who give advice about immigration, employment, health care, visas, and many other issues
- induction programmes to help you settle into your new surroundings
- meeting and greeting you at the airport when you first arrive
- international societies that organise trips and events.

If English is not your first language, ask prospective universities if they offer English language support classes before and during the academic year (and whether they are free or not).

Living costs, financial assistance and accommodation

Tuition fees vary between courses, and some courses are longer (and therefore more expensive) than others. Also, the cost of living varies widely between areas. Other things to think about include the availability of part-time work (and whether the university offers assistance to help you find it), and any university restrictions on working. Universities provide funding through scholarships and bursaries, although they are competitive and need to be applied for 1-2 years before the course begins. Check whether the university offers accommodation, the types available, and if they guarantee a place for international students (see Chapter 2). You can also work out how much money you need to live at different universities. Chapter 4 provides guidance about living and study costs and how to estimate them.

The British Council and UKCOSA

A lot of information is available from the British Council, which is an organisation that provides details about educational opportunities in the UK. It has offices around the world that provide advice about a range of topics, such as different types of courses and universities, how to fund your studies, visas, work, internships, etc. They provide information about UK culture and life and organise campaigns to attract international students. Further details are available from their website.

Another organisation you will find helpful is UKCOSA, which is the country's national advisory body concerning international students. They provide advice to international students about a wide range of issues, and produce a comprehensive set of guidance notes. Visit their website to learn more about them and how they can help you.

Making a decision

After reading this chapter, you will be aware of the different aspects to think about when choosing a course. Take your time and choose carefully. Make a shortlist of universities and courses that best match your needs, and then consider each one in detail. As you find out about different options, you can use the checklist on pp. 16–17 to remind you of the important points to bear in mind.

Also, UCAS provides two questionnaires (called the Stamford Test, and Centrigrade) that allow you to match your abilities and interests to subjects. They are available from the UCAS website.

Applying for a course

After you have carefully chosen a university and course, the next step is to apply. The application process differs for undergraduate and postgraduate courses.

Undergraduate courses

Applications for most full-time undergraduate courses (e.g., foundation degrees, HNDs, and bachelor degrees) are processed by the Universities and Colleges Admissions Service (UCAS), which is a centralised application process. Some courses,

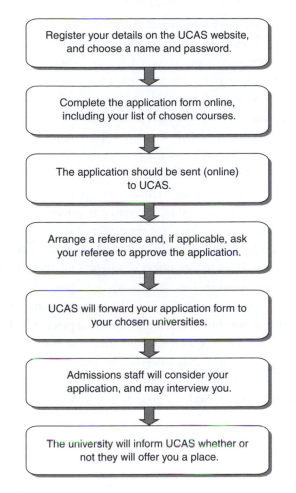

Register your details on the UCAS website, and choose a name and password.

Complete the application form online, including your list of chosen courses.

The application should be sent (online) to UCAS.

Arrange a reference and, if applicable, ask your referee to approve the application.

UCAS will forward your application form to your chosen universities.

Admissions staff will consider your application, and may interview you.

The university will inform UCAS whether or not they will offer you a place.

The UCAS application process

such as part-time programmes, have a different application process, and you should contact the relevant university for details.

Applications via UCAS begin in September. It is advisable to apply as early as possible because courses can become full, and some universities do not consider later applications. Also, you will need time for visa applications, to make arrangements to travel to the UK, perhaps attend a preparation (summer) class, or arrange funding. Note that Cambridge and Oxford, and medicine, dentistry, and art and design courses elsewhere require early applications. The closing date for applications from students resident in the UK/EU differs from students resident in other countries. Visit the UCAS website to see the closing dates.

All applications take place online. If you are currently studying as an international student in a British school or college, or at an overseas school registered with UCAS, your school will help with your application. If not, you should apply yourself, by completing an application form on the UCAS website. There is an application fee, which must be paid online using a credit or debit card. If you do not have Internet access, your local British Council office may be able to provide it.

After you complete your application, UCAS will send the details to the universities you listed on the application form. An Admissions Tutor for each course will consider your details, and will decide whether or not to offer you a place. This process takes about one to two months. You can track the progress of your application on the UCAS website. An Admissions Tutor will send their decision to UCAS, and they will then forward it to you. If a university decides to offer you a place, it will be either 'unconditional', which means you have satisfied the entry requirements and can attend the university, or 'conditional', if you have not yet achieved them. Alternatively, a university could decide to decline your application. When you have received a reply from all of your choices, you can decide which offers to accept. Only two choices are allowed – a first choice and an insurance choice.

If you receive a conditional offer but later do not achieve the entry requirements, contact the university to see if they will still offer you a place. UCAS offers an option called 'UCAS Extra' for students who have no offer (for example, if all their choices were rejected, or they declined all their offers). This option allows the choice of an additional course. The service ends in June. In August and September, there is a service called Clearing, which enables students who do not have a place to apply for courses that still have vacancies.

Completing the UCAS application form

Admission tutors at universities and colleges will use the information you provide in your UCAS application to make a decision about whether or not to offer you a place.

The UCAS form requires the following:

- personal details (e.g., your name, date of birth, address, and ethnic background)
- choice of courses (you can choose up to six courses, or four if you are applying for medicine, dentistry, or veterinary medicine)
- details about your secondary education experience
- qualifications you have, or expect to achieve, before the course begins
- details about your previous employment
- a personal statement
- a reference from your teacher, head teacher, or employer.

Personal statement

A personal statement is a personal essay that should explain your reasons for choosing the course and area of study; why you find them interesting; your interests relevant to the subject; your career aspirations; your previous work experience (particularly if relevant to your course); and other areas of achievement. You can also mention your hobbies and interests, and the skills they enabled you to develop (e.g., meeting deadlines, communication skills, problem solving, and self-motivation).

Reference

The application should be supported by a reference. The referee should be someone who knows you well and can therefore comment on your ability for higher education. The referee can be a teacher, head teacher, or employer, but cannot be a family member, relative, or friend.

Tips

- complete all required sections, and follow the instructions
- pay attention to detail
- make sure there are no grammar and spelling mistakes
- be honest when you write the personal statement
- don't include irrelevant information.

Further help

If you need help to complete the UCAS application form, you can contact UCAS, the Admissions Office at universities, your teacher or careers advisor, and your local British Council office. Some universities may have an office or representative in your country. There are also books available to help you complete the form.

Postgraduate courses

There is no centralised application process for postgraduate courses, except for PGCE programmes that are handled by the Graduate Teacher Training Registry (GTTR). Applications for other programmes should be made directly to the university you want to study at; each one has its own application process, form, and closing dates. An application pack can be requested from the university. The application form requires your personal details, your qualifications and experiences, a personal statement, and a reference. On the personal statement you can highlight your reasons for wanting to study the course, your previous academic successes, and relevant work experience.

There are three main types of postgraduate degrees: taught courses, research degrees, or a mixture of both. Taught courses have some similarities to undergraduate degrees because they involve modules and units, a variety of teaching and assessment methods, and a dissertation and exams. Taught courses include postgraduate certificates, postgraduate diplomas, and Master degrees.

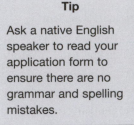

> **Tip**
>
> Ask a native English speaker to read your application form to ensure there are no grammar and spelling mistakes.

The second type of course, a research degree (e.g., MPhil or PhD), requires little attendance in formal lectures. They require an in-depth investigation of a topic and are supervised by two academic staff. During a research degree you will attend seminars about research methods, review the literature about a topic, collect and analyse data, and write a thesis. There are also professional doctorates, which involve research activities in the workplace, alongside taught courses. A new course is the 'New Route PhD', which combines interdisciplinary courses with a research project.

If you plan to study for a research degree, you should identify an area of study, and contact a potential supervisor. It is best to find out as much as you can about potential supervisors, including their research area, reputation and international profile, research quality, published work, and whether you would be studying alone or as part of a research team. Consider reading their previous research reports, and ask former research students about their experiences. The availability of funding is another issue to consider. See Chapter 7 for more about research degrees and how to find a suitable supervisor.

☑ What do you want from a course and university?

There are many factors to consider when choosing the right place to study

Course characteristics
- ☐ Subject that interests you
- ☐ Course you will be good at
- ☐ Course duration
- ☐ Career opportunities
- ☐ Vocational or academic course
- ☐ Teaching & assessment methods
- ☐ Entry requirements
- ☐ English language requirements
- ☐ Suitablity for international students
- ☐ Recognised in your country

Facilities, support, and social life
- ☐ Libraries and computers
- ☐ Sporting facilities
- ☐ Catering facilities
- ☐ Health and dental services
- ☐ Counselling and advisory services
- ☐ Places for religious worship
- ☐ Services for disabled students
- ☐ Guaranteed accommodation
- ☐ Student groups and societies

Reputation and quality
- ☐ Position in league tables
- ☐ Old or new university
- ☐ Teaching quality
- ☐ Research quality
- ☐ Student satisfaction
- ☐ Employability of recent graduates

Support for international students
- ☐ International student advisors
- ☐ Induction programme
- ☐ Airport meet-and-greet
- ☐ English language support
- ☐ International societies

Location and size
- ☐ Rural or urban
- ☐ City or suburbs
- ☐ Number of students
- ☐ Availability of amenities
- ☐ Transport links

Finances
- ☐ Tuition fees
- ☐ Cost of living
- ☐ Availability of part-time work
- ☐ Financial support
- ☐ Assistance to find part-time work

2 Leaving home and arriving in the UK

INTRODUCTION

After reading this chapter, you should be able to:

- ☑ Prepare for your life in the UK
- ☑ Understand the formalities to follow at the airport
- ☑ Know what to expect during your first week at university
- ☑ Arrange accommodation
- ☑ Settle in to the UK and overcome culture shock

This chapter helps you to prepare and plan for your arrival in the UK. There is an overview of the arrangements to make before leaving your country, and what to expect at the airport and during the first week at university. There are also suggestions for settling in and overcoming culture shock, and finding a suitable place to live.

Ten Things to do before leaving

Make arrangements before you leave your country. Begin by reading all of the information sent to you by your university. Make a note of important dates, such as enrolment on courses, payment of tuition fees, when to apply for accommodation, etc. It is also a good idea to learn about the country's culture and higher education system (see Chapters 7, 8 and 9). Below is a list of some preparations you may need to make.

1   Obtain a valid passport and/or national identity card (it could take several weeks or months to do this). Check whether you need a visa or entry clearance, and find out about other types of documents you will need to show the Immigration Officer when you arrive.

2   Find out if you need to have a health certificate, vaccinations, and a chest x-ray.

3   Plan your journey. It is advisable to buy travel insurance to cover yourself and belongings. Also consider purchasing other types of insurance, such as personal belongings insurance, to cover items while you are in the UK, and health insurance

to cover against medical expenses. See Chapter 6 to find out more about health care in the UK.

4   Inform the university about your arrival date and time, and ask them if they are willing to meet you when you arrive at the airport. Remember to take the telephone number of the university's International Support Office in case they need to be contacted during your journey.

5   Learn about the UK's customs regulations and the airline's baggage allowance.

6   Find out how to transfer your money to the UK, and whether your country has restrictions on the amount of money that can be transferred. If you need to apply for a scholarship, it is common to apply many months before the course begins.

7   Apply for university accommodation as soon as you have been accepted onto your course. If you prefer to live in private rented housing, you can book a temporary place to stay (e.g., a hotel, guesthouse, or bed and breakfast) while you search for somewhere permanent.

8   Learn about the UK, including its culture, and higher education system. You can also read about and prepare for culture shock and how to overcome it.

9   If English is not your first language, you can consider improving your language and study skills while you are waiting for your course to begin. This book is a good place to start as it provides details of the English language requirements (see next chapter) and has self-evaluation checklists to help you identify the skills that you need to improve. Colleges in your country offer intensive English courses. Another option is to read a few of the textbooks that will be used on your course in order to become familiar with their content and level.

10 The British Council organises programmes to inform students about immigration, visas, and other aspects of studying. Contact your local British Council office for details.

Items you should take to the UK

There are several items you should take to the UK. They include:

- Your passport and any required entry clearance (visa).
- Documents for immigration control. Keep photocopies separate from the originals. Passport-sized photographs also will be useful.
- Details about your travel arrangements and insurance.
- A map, instructions about how to reach your university, and contact details of the International Support Office.
- Enough money (about £200–300) to cover your immediate needs on arrival (e.g., customs charges, travel expenses to university, etc). More money will be needed if there is a delay opening your bank account or converting foreign currency. For safety reasons, do not carry large amounts of cash, and keep your money in a safe place, such as in an inside pocket or money belt.

- Make a note of the details of your travellers' cheques (e.g., serial numbers) in case they are stolen.
- Original or certified copies of your previous qualifications, and other documents to show the university.
- Enough clothing and essential items for your journey and first week.
- Although you can buy most items in the UK, you may want to bring things from your country, such as bed linen, souvenirs, or posters for your room.
- Consider leaving valuable items at home; if you do decide to take them, be careful!

> **Tip**
>
> Keep your passport, documents, travel tickets and cash in a safe place. Put immigration documents in your hand luggage so that they can be accessed easily.

Packing your belongings

Find out about customs regulations and baggage allowances. Customs regulations are the rules about the things you are allowed to take to the UK. Some goods are prohibited or restricted, whereas others require the payment of duties or tax. Further information about the types of goods you can take is available from HM Revenue and Customs. It is important to check the details before you leave your country; if you take illegal or forbidden items to the UK, there could be a heavy fine or even jail!

A baggage allowance is the amount of luggage you are allowed to take on to the plane. The allowance is usually 20kg, and there will probably be a surcharge for additional baggage. Remember to label your luggage.

If you decide to take electrical equipment, check that it is compatible with the UK electricity system. Electrical appliances in the UK use 240 volts, 50Hz, and three-pin square plugs. You may be able to buy an adaptor and voltage converter so that goods in your country can be used.

Arriving in the UK

Your university can provide advice about when you should travel. Courses begin in September or October, although you may want to attend a pre-sessional programme before your course begins to help you settle in to the UK, improve your English skills, and prepare for academic life (see the next chapter).

Most international students travel to the UK by plane, and arrive at an international or regional airport. Alternatively, if you are in Europe, you can travel either by the Eurostar to London, or via a ferry to a channel port (e.g., Dover, Harwich, Hull, Portsmouth or Southampton).

Entry clearance

People from certain countries need permission, known as an entry clearance or visa, from the British Government to enter the UK. It is advisable to check if you need entry clearance, and to apply for it as early as you can. The rules depend on your nationality, type and duration of the course, and other factors. There are different rules for citizens of the European Economic Area countries (or of Switzerland) and nationalities of other countries. Carefully check the immigration rules that apply to you.

- You can apply for entry clearance at your nearest British Embassy, High Commission, or Consulate General in your country.
- Up-to-date information about visa regulations are available from the Home Office (UK visas or the Border and Immigration Agency). The UK visas website has a questionnaire to help you determine if you need a visa. Residents in selected countries can also make online visa applications on the website.

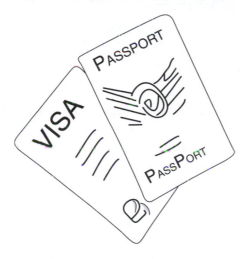

To apply for entry clearance, you will need to submit an application form, passport photographs, a fee, and documents to fulfil immigration conditions. Documents you need may include:

- Proof that you have been accepted on to a course
- Evidence to show that you can financially support your study
- Evidence of your qualifications, including your English language ability.

Rules about immigration and entry clearance are updated often and you should check them even if you think you do not need to. Anyone accompanying you

> **Tip**
>
> It would be convenient to arrive in the UK in the morning, to allow more time to reach your university, and to check-in to your accommodation.

to the UK (e.g., your spouse) should also check the rules. If you are refused entry clearance/visa, contact your university's International Support Office for advice.

At the airport or other point of entry, you will need to show the Immigration Officer that you meet the immigration requirements. Make a note of your visa's expiry date. You must either leave the UK before it expires, or apply for an extension at the Home Office (Border and Immigration Agency). It is advisable to apply for an extension a few months before the expiry date as the process takes time. Information is available from the Border and Immigration Agency, your university, and the Immigration Advisory Service.

At the airport

A popular way to travel to the UK is by plane. There is an extensive network of international airports located around the country. Your university will be able to give you details of the nearest one, and how to travel to the university from the airport. Major airports are located in the cities and areas listed below, and there are also regional airports.

- Aberdeen
- Belfast
- Bristol
- Birmingham
- Cardiff

- East Midlands
- Edinburgh
- Gatwick
- Glasgow
- Heathrow

- Leeds
- Luton
- Manchester
- Newcastle
- Stansted

After you arrive in the UK, you should leave the plane and follow the signs in the airport for 'Arrivals' (alternatively, if you are transferring to another plane, you should follow the signs for 'Flight connections'). You will need to pass through immigration control, collect your luggage, and then proceed to Customs. The final step of the journey is to travel from the airport to your university. Make a note of your flight number as you will need it to locate your luggage and find the correct queue at Customs.

STEP 1: Immigration control
At immigration control you will need to show that you meet the immigration requirements. An Immigration Officer will interview you and ask questions about your planned stay in the

country. The interview may take some time, and you could be asked to complete a routine health check at the airport. The Immigration Officer may ask to see documents such as:

- your passport and/or national identity card
- a visa/entry clearance (if required)
- a letter from your university that confirms you will study there
- evidence that you have sufficient funds for your tuition fees and living expenses (e.g., a bank statement or letter from sponsor)
- a medical certificate (if necessary).

Make sure you join the correct queue; otherwise you will waste a lot of time. Before you leave your country, find out about the immigration requirements, including the documents you will need to show the Immigration Officer.

Entry clearance is unlikely to be refused if you have the relevant documents, satisfy the immigration requirements, and can answer the Immigration Officer's questions satisfactorily. If you satisfy the immigration regulations, the Immigration Officer will put a stamp in your passport that states when you entered the UK.

It could also state the length of time you are allowed to stay, and other immigration conditions. Check the details of the stamp while you are at immigration control; inform the Immigration Officer if they are not correct. Note that if you arrive in the UK via the Eurostar, some of the immigration and customs checks may take place on the train.

If you encounter a problem at Immigration, you can ask the Immigration Officer to telephone your university, and request to see a representative of the Immigration Advisory Service.

STEP 2: Luggage collection and customs check

The next step is to collect your luggage, which will be unloaded from the plane onto a carousel in the baggage collection area. The carousel can be located by looking for the flight number which should be displayed above it. It is a good idea to label your luggage before your journey so that it can be easily located. If any of your luggage is lost or damaged, immediately report to the airline's office or representative at the airport.

When you have collected your belongings, next take them to Customs. Most UK airports and ports have three different customs exits (also known as 'channels'):

- *Green and Blue Channels.* If you have nothing to declare (no prohibited or restricted goods, and no more than the customs allowances), use either the Green channel (if you are travelling from outside the EU), or the Blue channel (if you are travelling from another EU country).
- *Red Channel.* Use the Red channel if you have either goods to declare, commercial goods, more than the customs allowances, or if you are unsure about what to declare.

(Continued)

STEP 3: Traveling from the airport to your university

After leaving the airport, you will need to travel to your university. This should be planned in advance. If you are going to study in London, you can arrive at a London airport (Gatwick, Heathrow, or Stansted) and travel to the university via public transport. For a university outside London, you can take a flight to the nearest airport. Some universities and scholarship agencies may arrange to send a representative to meet you at the airport and take you to the university. If not, ask them for information about how to get there by public transport. If you arrive at the airport late in the evening, or far from the final destination, it may be more convenient to stay in temporary accommodation overnight (e.g., a hotel or bed and breakfast), and then continue the journey the next day.

Before you leave the airport, you may want to change currency, and telephone your parents to let them know you arrived safely! Currency can be changed at Bureaux de Change centres located in international airports, ports and in some train stations.

If a problem arises during your journey, telephone your university for advice. Also, most entry ports have information centres.

Your first week at university

The first week at university will be a busy and exciting experience! As well as settling into a new country, you will need to pay your course fees, register and enrol on to courses, register with the local police and doctor, open a bank account, and maybe search for somewhere to live! There will be many social events during the first week where you can make friends and have fun.

Induction and orientation

The university will arrange induction and orientation programmes. They introduce new students to the university, campus, and other students. There may also be an induction programme specifically for international students. Also, the Student Union will organise a Freshers' Fair, which is a programme of social events where you can learn about student clubs and societies, as well as local companies, services, and community groups.

Finding your way around the campus

It is a good idea to obtain a map of the campus and surrounding area, and to go and explore it! During your first few days, you can:

- learn the names of the main university buildings
- find the location of your department and lectures
- read the notice boards in your department
- visit the library, and tour the library facilities
- plan the route from your home to your lectures
- explore the local town or city
- find out about local transport, shopping centres, super-markets, food outlets, and social events.

> **Tip**
>
> Visit a local tourist information centre for details about local attractions, events, restaurants, shops, and guesthouses.

Registering with the local police

You may need to register at a police office (or with the Overseas Visitors Records Office if you become a resident in the Metropolitan Police District in London). The requirement to register with the police will be stamped in your passport at Immigration Control. There is a time limit for registration, so try to do it within a few days of your arrival. The university will be able to provide details of the place you need to register at. Take your passport and passport-sized photographs to the police station, along with a fee. Remember to inform the police every time you change your address or status or extend your permission to stay in the country.

Opening a bank account

Several large banks offer accounts and services for students. It is more convenient to open an account at a branch in or near your campus. Before opening an account, it is a good idea to compare the benefits of each bank account, such as their interest rates, overdraft facilities, and Internet and international banking facilities. Chapter 4 contains advice about bank accounts and how to open one.

☑ Preparing for your arrival in the UK

There are many things you can do to prepare for your arrival in the UK

Before you leave

- ❐ Read all of the information sent to you by your university
- ❐ Make a note of important dates such as enrolment, fee payment, etc.
- ❐ Obtain a valid passport and, if applicable, entry clearance/visa
- ❐ Find out about the documents you will need to show at Immigration

(Continued)

☐ Check whether you need a health check and medical certificates
☐ Plan your journey to and within the UK
☐ Inform the university of your arrival day/time
☐ Find out about customs regulations
☐ Find out about how to transfer money to the UK
☐ Apply for university accommodation
☐ Learn about the UK, its culture, and higher education system
☐ Improve your English language skills

After you arrive
☐ Pass through Immigration and Customs
☐ Change foreign currency
☐ Travel to your university
☐ Book in to your accommodation (either temporary or longer term)
☐ Attend the university's induction and orientation programmes
☐ Tour the university and its facilities
☐ Attend the Freshers' Fair and other social events
☐ Register with the local police
☐ Open a bank account

Finding somewhere to live

Most universities provide accommodation for their students, which is usually a room in a student dormitory (Halls of Residence). Many universities guarantee a place for international students. It is common for students to live in a university-owned place in their first year, and then rent private accommodation in the second and third years. University-owned accommodation is probably most suitable if you are going to the UK for the first time.

Apply for a place as early as possible because there may be limited rooms and early closing dates for applications (it is best to apply as soon as you have been accepted onto a course).

An alternative option is to rent private-owned housing from a landlord or housing organisation.

University-owned accommodation

Universities provide a range of accommodation for students (Table 2.1). The most common type is a room in a Halls of Residence, which is popular among international and first-year students. It is a single room with a bed, wardrobe, desk, chair, and shared or private bathroom and kitchen facilities. Residences either provide cooked meals (known as 'catered accommodation'), or you are expected to buy and prepare your own meals (self-catering). Other types of housing include flats and houses. If your family are going to accompany you to the UK, your university might be able to provide suitable accommodation.

Every university will have an accommodation or housing office that provides guidance about finding a place to live. You can apply for a place by filling in an application form available from them (you might also need to pay a deposit).

There are several questions to think about when considering whether university – or private-owned accommodation is suitable for you:

- What is the size of the room?
- Is it catered or self-catered?
- Is the Halls of Residence single or mixed sex?
- How far is it from the university?
- How much privacy is there?
- How much is the rent, and what are the payment arrangements?
- Does the rent include meals, electricity, water, and gas bills?
- What is the length of the contract? Can students stay in the accommodation during the vacations?
- Is it furnished or unfurnished?

How do I find private accommodation?

If you want to arrange somewhere in the private sector, it is much easier to do so after you arrive. This also means you can visit potential properties to assess their suitability. You can stay in temporary accommodation (such as a hotel, guesthouse, or a bed and breakfast) while you search for a more permanent place. It can be booked in advance (ask the university accommodation office if they can help you to make a booking or if they offer temporary accommodation). The main types of private housing include:

- *Flats and houses*. A common option is for a group of 4/5 students to rent a flat or house together.
- *Bed sits*. One room in a house or larger building that serves as a bedroom and living room. Bathroom and kitchen facilities are shared or private.
- *Hostel*. A shared room in a large building run by a charity.
- *Home stay (lodgings)*. A room in a family home in which you live as part of the household.
- *Student accommodation*. Many universities have entered into partnership with private companies to offer privately-owned accommodation near campus.

The ease of finding accommodation varies between towns, cities, and even postcodes! It is particularly difficult and expensive to find a place to rent in certain areas in London. You can get an idea of prices and availability by looking on the Internet.

The university's accommodation office should be able to provide a list of places available in the private sector. You can also look in:

- an accommodation agency or other providers
- a local newspaper
- adverts on university notice boards
- friends and relatives living in the area
- the Student Union

To use an accommodation agency, you will need to register your name to get a list of properties. The accommodation agency should only charge a fee if they find accommodation for you.

Tenancy agreements

Private-owned accommodation is rented from a landlord or accommodation agency. They will ask you to sign a contract (also known as a 'tenancy agreement' or a 'lease'). It is a legally binding agreement; once you sign it, you are obliged to follow the conditions in it. Also note that legally-binding contracts must also be signed by students for university-owned accommodation. If you don't understand or agree to the agreement, seek advice from your university's accommodation office, Student Union, or local Citizens' Advice Bureau.

A group of students who rent a property together may be asked to sign a joint contract. This means that everyone is responsible for the rent and upkeep of the

Table 2.1   Types of student accommodation

Type	Description	Advantages	Disadvantages
Halls of Residence, or other accommodation owned by the university.	Usually includes a single bedroom, with either shared or private en-suite bathroom facilities. The housing is owned and managed by the university.	• Easy to make friends. • Rent usually includes water and electricity, and sometimes meals. • There are facilities such as washing machines. • Health and safety checks, and a security service. • Usually in a convenient location, and close to the university. • Easier to arrange in advance.	• Limited space & less independence. • Fixed term contract. • Some facilities (e.g., kitchen, and communal areas) are shared with other students. • Some universities do no permit residence during the summer. • Friends may not be allowed to stay overnight. • May be noisy.
Private Halls of Residence.	Owned by a private company. May be managed by the company, or the university.	• As above.	• As above.
Private sector accommodation.	Rented from the owner. May be a room, flat, bed sit, or house. A group of 4 or 5 students may rent a house together.	• More choice. • Independence. • Can share with friends. • May be cheaper than university accommodation.	• May need to pay rent during vacations, even if not resident. • Bills are not included in the rent. • If you share with friends, may have joint responsibility for the contract.
Lodgings.	A single room in a family home. You may be able to live as part of the household.	• Usually lower rent. • A fixed-term agreement may not be necessary. Useful for short-term accommodation. • A family atmosphere.	• Less independence. • There may be house rules. • Facilities are shared with the family. • Less security; you may be asked to leave at short notice.

property. It is important to choose your housemates carefully, as a joint contract means that you will have to pay if one or more of them does not pay their rent or damages the property.

There are different types of tenancy agreement:

- *Assured Shorthold Tenancy Agreement*. The most common type of tenancy agreement. It gives certain rights during the duration of the agreement; for example, the landlord cannot ask you to leave during the tenancy (without going to court), and the rent is usually fixed during the contract.
- *Assured Tenancy Agreement*. This type of agreement can be long-term. The landlord can increase the rent after the fixed term. Seek advice before you sign this type of agreement.
- *Contractual Tenancy Agreement*. Different rules apply if you live in the same property as the landlord (i.e., lodgings). There is limited security because the landlord can ask you to leave at short notice.

The tenancy agreement will contain the name and address of the landlord, details about the property, the length of the tenancy, details of the deposit and rent, and the responsibilities of you and your landlord.

On the next page is a reminder of the things to consider before signing a tenancy agreement.

Deposits, Insurance, and Council Tax

In addition to paying rent, you will need to pay a deposit, purchase insurance for your belongings, and check whether you need to pay Council Tax. The deposit is paid to the landlord to cover any damage that could be caused during the tenancy, or non-payment of rent. It is usually equivalent to four to six weeks' rent, and it is paid in advance of moving in.

It is advisable to purchase insurance for your personal possessions in case they are damaged or stolen. Insurance policies specifically for students may also cover the payment of tuition fees if you become ill or have an accident.

Council Tax is a property tax that tenants should pay to the local council to contribute towards public services. Full-time students are, in general, exempt from paying the tax, and you should check your eligibility with your university and local council. If you are exempt, you will need to fill in a Council Tax Discount and Exemption Form available from the university or local council.

☑ Before you sign the tenancy agreement ...

There are several things to think about before you sign the tenancy agreement

Tenancy agreement

- ☐ Do you understand and agree to all the points in the tenancy agreement?
- ☐ Have you shown the tenancy agreement to your university?
- ☐ Will you be given a duplicate copy of the agreement?
- ☐ Does the length of the tenancy meet your requirements?
- ☐ What should you do if something in the property needs repairing? Who will pay for it to be repaired?

Rent

- ☐ How is the rent collected? What does the rent include?
- ☐ Is the rent reduced during the vacation?
- ☐ How does the rent compare to other properties in the area?
- ☐ How much is the deposit? It is usually equivalent to one/two months' rent.
- ☐ Have you agreed an Inventory? If so, check it carefully. If not, ask your landlord for one.

Property

- ☐ Have you inspected the interior and exterior of the property? Is it clean and in a good state of repair?
- ☐ Do the gas, water, and electricity supplies work?
- ☐ Who is responsible for maintaining the garden?
- ☐ Does the landlord provide insurance for your personal belongings?

Safety

- ☐ Does the landlord have a certificate (Gas Safety Certificate) to show that a CORGI-registered gas engineer has annually checked the gas appliances?
- ☐ Does the landlord have certificates to indicate that electrical appliances and wiring are safe?
- ☐ Is the house equipped with a fire and burglar alarm, and smoke detectors?
- ☐ Have you checked the security of the property (e.g., do the doors and accessible windows have strong locks)?
- ☐ Does the furniture meet Safety regulations? They should have a label attached showing their compliance.
- ☐ Have previous tenants reported problems about the landlord to your university accommodation office?

After you move in

There are several things you should do after you move into your new home:

- Obtain receipts for any money you have given the landlord.
- Take readings of the water, electricity and gas meters, and inform the utility companies that you have moved in.
- Contact the telephone company to connect the telephone. Check to see that all appliances are working; if not, inform your landlord.
- Purchase a television licence if you need one.
- Complete the inventory (an inventory is a list of items in the property and their condition).
- Check whether you need to pay Council Tax, and consider taking out Home Insurance.
- Introduce yourself to the neighbours!

The responsibilities of you and your landlord

You and your landlord both have responsibilities during the duration of the tenancy agreement. Your responsibilities usually include:

- following the conditions in the tenancy agreement and paying your rent on time
- not damaging the property
- taking care of minor maintenance (e.g., replacing the light bulbs, putting out the garbage, etc)
- locking the windows and doors when you go out
- obtaining written permission from the landlord if you want to make alterations to the property.

Your landlord's responsibilities usually include:

- ensuring that the property is safe
- keeping the structure and exterior of the property (e.g., roof, windows) in good repair
- repairing the structure and exterior of the building, as well as the bath, toilets, sinks, heating, and electrical wiring
- giving reasonable notification before entering the property (e.g., 24 hours)
- following the conditions in the tenancy agreement.

What should I do if I have a problem with the landlord?

Both you and the landlord should abide by the terms of the tenancy agreement. However, a number of students have problems with their landlords. Common complaints include:

- unwillingness to carry out repairs
- entering the property unannounced
- trying to increase the rent
- not returning the deposit.

If you encounter a problem you can initially discuss it with the landlord or letting agency. If the problem is not resolved, the next step is to write a letter to the landlord to explain the problem and request a solution. If the letter does not help, you should seek advice from the university accommodation office, Student Union or Citizen's Advice Bureau. Never refuse to pay rent; otherwise, the landlord can take legal action against you. It is a good idea to keep a written record of the landlord's behaviour, as well as the action you take to try to remedy the situation.

When you leave the property

The property must be in a clean and good condition when you leave at the end of the tenancy agreement. If not, the landlord can deduct money from your deposit to clean the property or to repair damaged items. Below are things to check before vacating:

- clean the rooms, including the kitchen and the bathroom
- do not leave rubbish in the property
- inform the utility and phone companies that you will leaving, and take readings of the meters
- repair any damage that you caused during your stay
- return all of the keys.

Culture shock

Don't be surprised if you have initial difficulties adjusting to life in the UK. It can be stressful to leave your home and settle into a new country and culture. The UK's climate, food, language, behaviour and social traditions may, at first, seem strange, confusing, and uncomfortable. This problem is common and is known as 'culture shock'. It occurs because the habits, customs, and lifestyle in a new country conflicts with the cultural values in your country. Don't worry – culture shock is a normal and temporary experience that many students experience. Below are common feelings you could experience after you arrive:

- *Conflict between two cultures*. It can be difficult to integrate your new experiences of the UK with your cultural values. British people's habits might not make sense, and you could feel hostile to them.
- *Homesickness and difficulty continuing relationships*. It can be difficult to keep in contact with your family and friends, and you may miss your country.
- *Frustration*. Communicating your thoughts and feelings to others can sometimes be difficult and frustrating.

There are four general stages of culture shock, although not everyone experiences each stage:

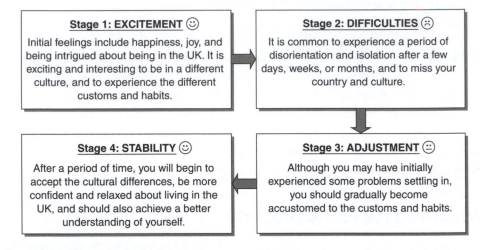

Four stages of culture stock

How can I overcome culture shock?

You should gradually begin to settle in to the UK. Below are suggestions to help the transition go smoothly:

- Know that culture shock exists and anticipate possible problems before you arrive. Make preparations to tackle culture shock, such as learning about the life and culture in the UK, and how it differs from your country.
- Accept that culture shock is part of the experience of living in a new country, and that it will take time to adjust.
- Be open-minded. Every country has strengths and weaknesses. Be patient; try to not criticise cultural differences, and do not blame yourself for any problems.
- Share your experiences with other people. For example, you can meet other students from your country. A good way to do this is to join the international students' society at your university.
- Appreciate the benefits of culture shock. It will increase your awareness of cultural and international issues, and also your sensitivity to people with different values and customs. You will also learn to work with people from other nationalities, which may be useful when returning to employment in your own country.
- Keep in touch with people at home, such as your parents, and let them know how you are feeling. There are other people who can offer support, including your friends, tutor, university counselling service, etc.
- Always keep a sense of humour! It is often better to laugh at irritations than become frustrated.

3 English language requirements for your course

INTRODUCTION

After reading this chapter, you should be able to:

- ☑ Know about English language entry requirements
- ☑ Understand The International Language Testing System (IELTS)
- ☑ Understand the features of Academic English
- ☑ Choose and use an English language dictionary

Courses in the UK are taught in English. This chapter describes the English language qualifications required for study at university, and the alternatives for students who do not have them. There is information about Academic English, the type of English language support you can expect to receive during your studies, and a guide to using an English dictionary.

English language qualifications

If English is not your first language, you may need to have an English language qualification to prove that you have a sufficient level. The preferred language test accepted by universities is the International English Language Testing System (IELTS), which is managed by the British Council and other organisations. A number of other qualifications from around the world, including the Test of English as a Foreign Language (TOEFL), are also accepted. Note, however, that a few universities or departments only accept IELTS and not alternatives. Contact your university for information about their requirements.

The university will need to see official certification or transcripts of your qualification, along with evidence of your other entry requirements (if the certificates are not in English, you will need to arrange for them to be translated). English language qualifications need to be recent, such as within the past two years. Many universities offer in-house English tests (i.e., tests they organise themselves), which they consider equivalent to (and therefore accepted in lieu of) the IELTS and other tests.

The IELTS score that you need depends on the course and university. The majority of undergraduate and postgraduate courses accept an IELTS score of 5.5–7.0, which is roughly equivalent to 213–250 on the computer-based TOEFL. Lower level courses, such as foundation programmes, have lower requirements, whereas others require higher scores. Check the entry requirements before you apply for a course.

Note that nationals of selected countries do not need to provide evidence of their English language ability. Also, some universities will be willing to waive the English language requirement for certain students whose academic record demonstrates their ability to study and be examined in English. Further, universities might admit students without an English language qualification on the condition that they complete an English course or test within a specified time.

The International English Language Testing System (IELTS)

The IELTS assesses whether non-native English speakers have sufficient English language skills to study and succeed on university courses. There are two versions of the test; the 'Academic module', for students who wish to study at university, and the 'General training' format for those who are going to the UK to work, attend a training programme, or complete secondary school. This chapter refers to the former.

Test structure

The IELTS probes the four basic language skills – listening, reading, writing, and speaking.

The listening paper examines listening skills in social and educational contexts. It includes recordings of a single speaker, conversations between two or more speakers, and a university lecture or talk. The passages cover a variety of accents and dialects, and increase in difficulty as they progress. Students are allowed to listen to the passages only once. A range of listening skills are assessed, including the ability to:

- listen for general and specific information
- listen for main ideas, details, and keywords
- understand gist
- understand speakers' opinions.

The reading part has three passages (between 2,000–2,750 words each) taken from non-specialist books, magazines, and newspapers. The reading skills that are assessed include the ability to:

- skim for general understanding
- scan for specific information

- identify writers' views, including a detailed argument
- understand how a process works
- use different written styles.

The writing paper consists of two tasks. The first task requires students to write a descriptive report (at least 150 words) based on data that is presented in a graph, table, or diagram. In task two, students must answer a short essay question (at least 250 words) that includes a point of view, argument, or problem. Writing skills that are checked in the test include the ability to:

- use appropriate content and vocabulary
- describe and explain data
- compare and contrast
- present a point of view or problem, with supporting evidence
- write in a variety of styles, and use a logical structure
- summarise main features
- discuss abstract issues and describe a process or how something works.

In the speaking section, there is a face-to-face interview with an examiner. Students are expected to answer short questions about themselves and their life, to speak at length about a familiar topic, and discuss issues and ideas. Speaking skills you need include:

- good pronunciation, intonation, and fluency
- ability to describe personal details and talk about everyday issues
- ability to express opinions and views and interact with the examiner
- keep the conversation flowing
- discuss topics

The listening, reading, writing, and speaking papers each have a different number of sections and questions (see Table 3.1). There is a range of question types, including multiple choice, short-answer questions, completion of sentences and diagrams, and choosing suitable paragraph headings.

Table 3.1

Module	Approximate test duration (minutes)	Number of tasks/sections	Number of questions
Listening	30*	4	40
Reading	60	3	40
Writing	60	2	2
Speaking	11–14	3+	variable

10 minutes is provided for students to transfer their answers to an answer book

How can I prepare for the IELTS test?

There are several things you can do to prepare for the test.

- *Apply for the test*. To apply to take the test, you will need to complete an application form and hand it in to the test centre along with passport-sized photographs and proof of identity.
- *Become familiar with the test*. Being familiar with the test format, including its structure and the types of tasks and questions, will enable you to focus more on your English skills to improve your score. Information about IELTS, as well as preparation notes and test materials, can be downloaded or purchased from the IELTS website.
- *Attend a preparation course*. Some colleges offer courses to coach students for the test. They explain the test system, provide practise, and offer mock tests and feedback.
- *Read books about the test*. There will be books in your local bookshop that are designed to help students prepare; they provide exam strategies and tips, vocabulary, practice tests, and model answers.
- *Identify the skills being tested*. As the IELTS examines certain English skills (not only English proficiency) in each question, try to identify those being tested, and demonstrate your ability at them.
- *Take a mock test*. Taking a mock test will help you to practise your exam skills and judge your current level.

Taking the IELTS test

The IELTS test can be taken at many places around the world; there are more than 300 centres in over 100 countries. Your teacher or college can let you know the nearest one. Most centres offer the test monthly. The Listening, Reading and Writing tests are taken on the same day, whereas the Speaking test is taken on the same day or a few days before or after. Previously, students had to wait three months before they could re-sit the IELTS test; now there are no restrictions.

In the exam room:

- *Attend on time*. Make sure that you know the date, time, and place of the test. Do not be late, otherwise you may not be allowed to take the test.
- *Take proof of identity*. You will need to show appropriate proof of identity. Check the type of identification that should be taken.

- *Read and listen to the rules and regulations.* Follow the exam instructions carefully, otherwise your test could be disqualified. Only take items that are permitted in the test room, such as a pen/pencil and eraser. Note that your mobile phone and other belongings should be placed outside the room. Do not talk to other candidates after the test has started.
- *Read the test paper carefully.* Read the instructions and questions so that you know what needs to be done and how. Ensure that you have the correct test format (i.e., the Academic module). Fill in the details required on the front of the paper.
- *Write your answer.* Take care when you write the answers. Poor spelling and grammar, and illegible handwriting may be penalised. For the listening and reading tests, make sure that you transfer your answers onto the Answer Sheet. If not, they will not be marked. Think carefully about the correct answer; for example, when filling in a blank, only write down the missing word(s) and write no more than the word limit. When writing an answer, do not copy sentences from the exam paper, use your own words to paraphrase the information and never go above the word limit.
- *Check your answers before you finish.* Check that your answers make sense and are grammatically correct. Do not take any test materials away from the room. If you have a problem, raise your hand and ask an invigilator for assistance.

There is general information about exams and study skills in Chapters 8 and 9.

Test results

The results are issued on a 'Test Report Form' by the centre thirteen days after the test. The form will also include your name, nationality, first language, and date of birth. Your performance will be rated as a score for each module, known as a Band Score, on a scale of 1 (non-user of English) to 9 (expert user). The four scores are then calculated to produce an 'Overall Band Score' (see Table 3.2). The band scores reflect the ability to use and understand English at university level.

The Band Score required for entry on to a course reflects the level of English language needed, as courses vary in their linguistic demands. In addition to the Overall Band Score, some courses require a certain score in a particular paper.

Test of English as a Foreign Language (TOEFL)

Another test is the TOEFL. It is managed by the Educational Testing Service in the USA, and is an American test of English as a foreign language in university settings.

Table 3.2

IELTS Band Scores and their meaning
9 Expert user
8 Very good user
7 Good user
6 Competent user
5 Modest user
4 Limited user
3 Extremely limited user
2 Intermittent user
1 Non-user
0 Did not attempt test

Many universities also accept TOEFL as an English language qualification; however, a number do not accept it, so you should check before applying. TOEFL has had different formats during recent years; the most commonly taken test is the Internet-based version, in which students answer questions using a computer at test centres. The precise format of the paper can differ depending on the country the student lives in.

Below is a rough comparison of TOEFL and IELTS scores to help you judge your level. However, there is no official comparison and it is not possible to match them precisely as the two tests have many differences, including the skills they test. For this reason, different universities will cite slightly different IELTS and TOEFL comparisons as entry requirements. Again, check with the university before you apply.

Table 3.3   A rough comparison of IELTS and TOEFL scores

IELTS Band	TOEFL score (internet-based test)
7.0	100
6.5	90
6.0	80
5.5	70
5.0	60
4.5	50

What if I don't have the English requirements?

There are several things you can do if you need to improve your English language skills before you start your course.

Study English!

Learn English intensively, either in your country or in the UK. The advantage of studying in the UK is that you will be surrounded by English all of the time! The amount of time you will need depends on you current level and also your ability to learn a language. A wide range of English courses – for all ages and levels – are available, and you can study at a private language school, college, or university. Your local British Council office will be able to provide details of accredited courses in the UK. Key points to consider when choosing a course include the level, number of class hours, class size, course fees, and accommodation costs.

Pre-sessional (or Pre-entrance) Programme

Universities offer short intensive English programmes for students who want to improve their language skills or for students who have been offered a place on a course but have narrowly missed the English Language requirement. Programmes are held 1–2 months before the beginning of the course (e.g., in the summer for a course that begins in September). They help students to:

- develop language skills
- improve vocabulary and grammar
- practise study skills
- learn about life in the UK.

Successful completion of the programme at a university usually satisfies the English language requirement of their degree courses (you should check if this is the case).

International Foundation Programme

An International Foundation Programme is a one-year course designed for students who have completed high school and want to increase their level of competence in the English language. Students whose high school qualifications do not meet the required level may also be able to take the course. The main focus of the course is to improve English Language and study skills; there may also be the option to specialise in a subject of your choice. Students who pass the course may be guaranteed a place on an undergraduate or postgraduate degree at the same university.

Pre-Masters programme

This course is similar to Pre-sessional and Foundation Programmes but focuses specifically on preparing students for Master degree level. The length of the course depends on your English language level and other qualifications.

Studying in English at university

The level of English used in university is different to conversational English. It is more demanding and complex. You will need to understand and discuss issues at a deeper level; express issues clearly and coherently; think critically about ideas; and use a variety of styles.

Before you begin your studies

You must have a standard of English that will enable you to benefit fully from the course. Therefore, it is very important to consider carefully whether your English level is sufficient (as already noted, you can find out your English ability by taking a test such as IELTS). Courses vary in the demands they make on your English; those that are linguistically demanding require a higher language ability. For example, some subjects in the humanities and social sciences may have a higher IELTS requirement than those in science, engineering, and mathematics.

English language support during your course

Universities provide English language support to their students, arranged in regular classes, workshops, language labs, or as individual tuition. They are likely to take place in a language centre or department. You may be asked to undertake an English test at the beginning of the semester to determine if you need language support and to assign you to an appropriate class. Bear in mind that not all universities offer free English language support.

Academic English (English for Academic Purposes)

English that is used in academic contexts is advanced and is known collectively as 'Academic English' or 'English for Academic purposes'. A good grasp of academic English is essential for success at university. The main features of Academic English are:

1 *Formal*. Academic English uses formal vocabulary and is free from grammar errors. The use of slang (informal words and expressions) and colloquialism (conversational expressions that are spoken by people every day) is avoided.

2 *Clear, concise and precise*. Academic English uses fewer words to express something and gets straight to the point. The argument and line of reasoning can be followed easily. Hesitation (e.g., er, um, well) is common in conversational English but not in university.

3 *Impersonal and objective*. Another feature of academic English is its impartiality, which means that it does not usually reflect your view. There should also be no bias and subjective reasoning. Instead of stating personal opinions, you should look for viewpoints in books, published articles, and other sources. Personal pronouns, such as 'I, me, my' are usually omitted.

4 *Logical structure and use of evidence*. There should be a clear and logical structure and progression between ideas. Sentences should link into paragraphs, and each paragraph should follow from the previous one. Arguments have an introduction; development of a main idea; a conclusion; and are supported by evidence and examples.

5 *Use of difficult and full words*. Shortened forms of words and phrases are common in spoken English, but avoided at university level. This includes abbreviations (a shortened form of a word or phrase) and contractions (words that have been shortened; e.g., 'it did not = didn't' and 'they are = they're'). Vocabulary used at university level tends to be more complex than that used in everyday language, and can include jargon (specialist or technical words).

6 *Generalisations and caution*. In academic English statements and conclusions are careful or tentative to make them less definite. This gives allowance for other people's viewpoints. It is also common to generalise (infer general comments) about something.

7 *Style*. Academic writing can follow different styles, such as descriptive, argumentative, and evaluative.

8 *References*. Academic work lists books, articles and other sources to show where the facts came from.

9 *Advanced skills*. During your studies you will develop a range of skills such as how to write assignments, listen to lectures, give presentations, read and summarise articles, etc. These skills are an integral part of using academic English.

Note that the distinction between academic and non-academic English is not always clear-cut. The characteristics described above are not always included in academic English, and usage and style varies across disciplines. For example, non-academic English can also be very formal.

Using an English language dictionary

A dictionary is a very useful tool to help you to study your course in English. A good dictionary will enable you to do the following:

- look up the meaning and spelling of a word
- translate a word you see or hear
- find several meanings of a word and how they fit a particular context

(Continued)

- know how to pronounce a word
- look up grammar usage
- find example sentences about how a word is used.

Choosing a dictionary

There are different types of dictionary, and each one has good and bad points. Your choice depends on your English level, and what you want the dictionary for. There are generally two types – an English–English dictionary that defines and explains words in English, and a bilingual dictionary for translating words. An English–English dictionary is better for finding English definitions and English phrases but it will not give the meaning in your first language. Below is a list of points to consider when choosing a dictionary:

- Level of difficulty.
- Number of words, phrases, and examples.
- Amount of detail for each word. Some dictionaries give short definitions, whereas others provide detail and give examples.
- Type of dictionary. (e.g., for general use; specific aspects of the English language such as idioms, verbs, pronouncing; or related to a degree subject).
- Monolingual or bilingual.
- Layout and structure
- Some dictionaries contain additional facts such as units of measurements and conversion scales.
- Size/weight. Some dictionaries are desk-size (large and heavy), whereas others are pocket-size.
- British or American English (or both). Obviously, a British English dictionary is suitable for studying in the UK.
- Price. Dictionaries vary in price.

Some dictionaries are designed specifically for advanced learners of English as a second language. They are likely to be more suitable for non-native speakers; they contain less complicated definitions, more example sentences, and commonly used words. Examples are:

- *Cambridge Advanced Learner's Dictionary*
- *Collins Cobuild Advanced Learner's English Dictionary.*
- *Oxford Advanced Learner's Dictionary*

Using a dictionary

Take time to familiarise yourself with your dictionary and to understand how it works. It is also a good idea to practise finding words quickly. Dictionaries are arranged in alphabetical order, and there are words printed at the top of each page to guide you to the correct page.

Meaning

Many English words have more than one meaning. When looking up a word, read through all of them and find the one that fits the situation and makes most sense. Go back to where you found the word – such as a textbook – and re-read the sentence or paragraph. It is good practice to keep a record of all new words that you come across and to write down details of its usage, such as collocations (words that often go together) and different forms (e.g., nouns, verbs, adjectives).

Spelling

To find the spelling of a word, you will need to know the first few letters. When you have checked it in the dictionary, look at variations of how the word is spelt. If you need to find out the English translation of a word in your own language, you may find that there is more than one translation. Do a back translation to check it. Some dictionaries list the frequency of each word (commonly and least commonly used words). Another useful tool is a thesaurus, which lists related words and concepts.

Examples

Some dictionaries provide sentences to show how words are used. They are useful because they give you some grammatical usage about a word, enable you to see if you understand its meaning and show how to use a word in sentences. They also help you to use correct English sentences.

Pronunciation

A good dictionary will have details (using a phonetic symbol system) about the pronunciation of a word. As there are various phonetic systems used around the world, choose a dictionary that uses one that you are familiar with (the International Phonetic Alphabet is a common system). Some dictionaries provide an explanation of the pronunciation system.

Electronic dictionaries

Many dictionaries are now electronic, either as a hand-held device, a CD-ROM, or an online version. They help to look up information quickly, and have additional functions such as recordings to help you pronounce a word, and photographs or movies to help explain concepts. However, they may not be allowed in exam halls.

An example of an entry

The figure on the next page illustrates the information given about a word in a typical dictionary. Each dictionary has a different layout, features and conventions, and there will be an introductory guide which explains how to use it.

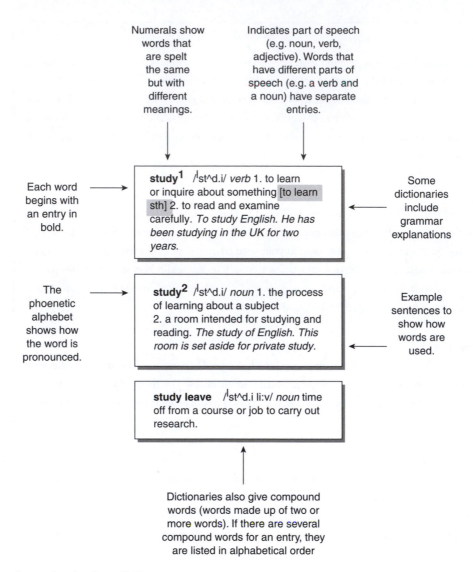

Numerals show words that are spelt the same but with different meanings.

Indicates part of speech (e.g. noun, verb, adjective). Words that have different parts of speech (e.g. a verb and a noun) have separate entries.

Each word begins with an entry in bold.

study¹ /ˈstʌd.i/ *verb* 1. to learn or inquire about something [to learn sth] 2. to read and examine carefully. *To study English. He has been studying in the UK for two years.*

Some dictionaries include grammar explanations

The phoenetic alphebet shows how the word is pronounced.

study² /ˈstʌd.i/ *noun* 1. the process of learning about a subject 2. a room intended for studying and reading. *The study of English. This room is set aside for private study.*

Example sentences to show how words are used.

study leave   /ˈstʌd.i liːv/ *noun* time off from a course or job to carry out research.

Dictionaries also give compound words (words made up of two or more words). If there are several compound words for an entry, they are listed in alphabetical order

A word entry in a dictionary

4 Tuition fees and living costs

INTRODUCTION

After reading this chapter, you should be able to:

☑ Identify the main costs of studying in the UK
☑ Know how to choose and open a bank account
☑ Use a budget to manage your finances
☑ Understand the UK currency and how to pay for goods

Studying in the UK offers good value for money as the quality of teaching is excellent and the qualifications are prestigious and recognised around the world. However, tuition fees and living expenses can be higher than in other countries. This chapter helps you to plan how much money you will need, learn how to pay for goods, and to choose and open a bank account. There is also advice about sources of financial support such as scholarships.

How much will it cost?

Before you go to the UK you must make sure that you have enough money to cover all of your study and living expenses. Be realistic about how much money your studies will cost and how much you can afford. Keep in mind that when you arrive in the country, you may be asked by immigration officers to show that you have enough funds to live on.

The total cost of living should take into account course fees, general living costs, and other costs. They include:

- tuition fees
- accommodation
- visa fees
- travel to and within UK
- food and other daily expenses

- books and course equipment
- social events and entertainment.

What are course fees?

Course fees – also known as tuition fees – cover the cost of the teaching and course materials you will receive, as well as exams, assessment, learning facilities and other university services. They do not include accommodation, travel and living costs, or the cost of textbooks. In addition to course fees, other fees are sometimes charged for items such as special equipment, field trips and English language tuition.

Cost

Course fees vary between courses and universities. They range from several thousand pounds to £25,000+, and are typically around £8,000–£11,000. Details of fees can be found in university prospectuses and websites. Classroom-based courses tend to have slightly lower fees than practical or vocational courses that involve workshop, laboratory or technology-based work. Short courses and foundation courses are the cheapest, whereas business and management postgraduate courses, particularly the MBA, can be expensive.

Universities keep their course fees fixed for the duration of their course, or raise them slightly each year in line with inflation. Part-time course fees are about half the price of the full-time equivalent, although they depend on the number of modules taken per academic year.

There are two common levels of course fees. Generally, tuition fees for nationals of countries in the European Economic Area (EEA) are likely to be classed as 'Home' fees (the same amount as for UK students), whereas students from outside the EEA usually pay a higher 'Overseas fee' because the UK government does not contribute towards it. However, the rules that determine which fee level you should pay are complicated, so you should contact your university for confirmation. They will ask you to complete a questionnaire and give details about yourself so that they can assess the amount you should pay.

When and how to pay

Course fees can sometimes be paid in instalments during the academic year, although a discount may be offered if the full amount is paid before or at enrolment. You will probably need to pay a deposit before you go to the UK, which could be non-refundable if you later decide not to study the course. Course fees can be paid by cash (in pound sterling), cheque, credit or debit card, bankers draft, or by a bank transfer.

Sources of funding

Before you study in the UK, you must have a reliable source of funding (this may be a condition of your immigration). Funding can come from a family member (e.g., parents), a sponsor, or a funding body in the UK or your country.

There are many scholarships and other awards for international students. Schemes can cover all tuition and living expenses, or offer a smaller contribution towards the total cost (which means that you cannot rely solely on a scholarship for funding). However, be warned that these are very competitive, and it is not easy to obtain a scholarship or other type of funding. Financial support is primarily offered by:

- the government or an organisation in the UK or your country
- a university.

Information about possible sources of funding is available from:

- Ministry or Department of Education in your country.
- The British Council. They provide a list of the main scholarship schemes, and their website has an online database to help you search for one.
- Individual universities.

> **Tip**
>
> Begin searching for scholarships as early as possible. You will need to apply early. It is almost impossible to arrange financial support after you arrive.

Check the details of scholarship schemes carefully, as they have strict criteria. For example, they could be only for students on certain courses, from certain countries, or below an age limit. Also, scholarships attract a large number of applicants and are competitive; they are often awarded on academic merit, which means that an excellent academic record is needed to be in with a chance of getting one.

Dealing with financial difficulties

If you encounter any financial problems in the UK, you can:

- talk to a student advisor
- ask your university if they can delay or extend your tuition fee payments
- universities have a 'hardship fund', which can provide short-term financial help for students with unexpected and unforeseen financial problems
- your local Citizen's Advice Bureau can give advice about how to manage debt
- a limited number of private trusts and charities offer small amounts of money.

Most international students are not eligible for welfare benefits from the UK government. Nationals from EU countries have some entitlements, and there could be temporary help for non-EU nationals in urgent cases. For more information, contact your local job centre.

If your financial problems are long-term, or extensive, then you may need to return to your country to raise funds; it may be possible to defer your course for a year.

Living costs and budgeting

Living in the UK can be more expensive than in other countries. Living costs vary, and depend on where you live and the standard of living you want. Certain cities are cheaper than others; London and other big cities are the most expensive. A guide to the price of various items is listed in Tables 4.1 and 4.2. Universities can also provide details about the cost of living in their local area.

Living costs vary from student to student. As a general guide, the cost of living for one year is about £7000 for an undergraduate student and £9000 for a postgraduate (several thousand extra is needed if you intend to live in London). Living costs will obviously be much higher if you intend to support a partner or child, own a car, stay in the UK during vacations, or travel around the UK and Europe. In addition, there will be initial costs such as travel to the UK, temporary accommodation while looking for a permanent place, registration with police, etc. Below is an outline of the estimated costs for a student for one academic year. The figures are presented as a guide only, and you should do more research before planning your costs.

Tip

Surf the websites of shops in the UK to learn more about prices of their products.

Table 4.1   Estimated living costs for one student in the UK

Item	Cost (£ per year)
Accommodation & household bills	3000–5000
Food	1500–2000
Clothing	300–400
Books and stationary	250–500
Telephone	200–250
Local transport	400–500
Social activities & leisure	1500
Other general living expenses	1500
Living expenses for a partner	3500–4000
Extra each year for a child	2500–3000

Table 4.2   Estimated price of various items in the UK

Item	Cost
Study	
Academic book	£30
Pen	£1
Writing paper	£2
A4 Ring binder	£2
Food	
Loaf of bread	50p
Chocolate bar	50p
Soft drink	50p
Cup of coffee	70p
Pint of milk	40p
Sandwich	£1.50
Sugar (500g)	60p
Butter (250g)	80p
Rice (2kg)	£1.30
Apples (1kg)	£1.20
Potatoes (1kg)	£1.80
Housekeeping & toiletries	
Washing powder	£3
Shampoo	£3
Toothpaste	£1.50
Wash laundry at a laundrette	£2
Clothes	
Coat	From £40
Trousers	From £20
Jumper	£20
Shirt	From £10
Shoes	£20–25
Skirt	£15–25
Haircut	£5–£20
CD	£15
Newspaper	20p–£1
Entertainment & social life	
Cinema ticket	£5–£8
Entry to nightclub	£10–£20
Pint of Beer	£2
Short bus or train trip	£1–£5

Creating a budget

It will help to plan how you are going to spend your money and manage your finances. One way to do this is to use a budget to predict your likely income and expenditure for each week, month, or year of the course.

Getting started

On the next page is a blank budget, and the following suggestions should help you get started.

1   Choose a timeframe. Decide whether you want to create a budget for each week, month and/or year.
2   Make a note of your expected income.
3   Think carefully about your expenses. Several can be recorded accurately, because they have a fixed price (e.g., course fees), whereas others will be approximate because they will vary monthly (e.g., food, clothes, household supplies, etc).
4   Choose how much detail will be included in the budget. The items listed on the next page are suggestions only – you can delete or add extra categories.
5   After you have estimated your costs, add them up and deduct them from your income. Make sure that you have enough money! If your expenditure is too high, think about how it can be reduced.

Evaluating the budget

Review and update your budget regularly. At the end of each week or month, compare your spending with your estimated costs. Keep track of your spending by saving receipts, details of ATM transactions, and looking at your bank statements.

Bear in mind that it is not possible to predict every expense you will need. The budget should be flexible, as changes will need to be made when your income or spending varies. A more accurate budget can be created after you are familiar with the cost of living.

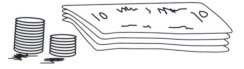

Money and banking

Currency

Currency in the UK is based on the pound sterling (£). One pound (£1) is made up of 100 pence (100p). Coins and notes commonly used include:

- Coins: 1p, 2p, 5p, 10p, 20p, 50p, £1, £2
- Notes: £5, £10, £20, £50, £100

In addition to the above, other bank notes are used in Scotland (which can be used in other parts of the UK), and the Channel Islands and Isle of Man issue different coins that are not commonly accepted elsewhere (although the pound sterling can be used there).

Tip

Coins and notes in the UK are different to those in your country. Also, some UK coins are similar. Take time to recognise the different coinage.

BUDGET PLANNER			
INCOME			
Item		*Amount of money*	
		Estimated	Actual
TOTAL INCOME			
EXPENDITURE			
Item		*Amount of money*	
		Estimated	Actual
Accommodation	Rent		
	Electricity/Gas/Water		
	Telephone		
	TV Licence		
	Household supplies		
	Laundry/dry cleaning		
	Insurance		
	Other		
Food	Groceries		
	Eating out		
	Other		

(Continued)

(Continued)

BUDGET PLANNER			
EXPENDITURE			
Item		*Amount of money*	
		Estimated	Actual
Personal items	Clothes		
	Hair styling		
	Toiletries		
	Music		
	Cigarettes		
	Other		
Study costs	Books		
	Stationary		
	Special equipment for course		
	IT costs (e.g., printing assignments)		
	Photocopying		
	English language support/exams		
	Field trips		
	Other		
Transport	Local transport (e.g., bus/train)		
	To the UK from your country		
	Visa		
	Other		
Social activities	Entertainment		
	Leisure activities		
	Sports		
	Gifts		
	Other		

BUDGET PLANNER			
EXPENDITURE			
Item		*Amount of money*	
		Estimated	Actual
Health care	Dentist		
	Optician		
	Medicine & Prescriptions		
	Health insurance		
	Other		
Emergency fund*			
Other			
TOTAL EXPENDITURE			
* Include an 'emergency fund' to help prepare for unexpected costs			

Money saving tips

There are several ways to save money during your daily life in the UK.

- Use the budget planner in this chapter to keep track of your expenses. Make a habit of reviewing your spending on a regular basis.
- Some shops and services offer discounts to students. You can also buy special discount cards to reduce the cost of certain services, such as travelling by train or coach.

(Continued)

- Compare prices in different shops. Supermarkets tend to be the cheapest and supermarket-labelled brands tend to cost much less than branded food. Ask other students for tips about where to shop.
- Look for discounted food and special offers in supermarkets. Food that is sold in bulk or has almost reached the best-before-date is reduced in price.
- To reduce household bills, always turn off lights and other appliances when they are not in use.
- It costs less to eat in university dining halls than in shops outside the campus, and it is cheaper to cook for yourself than to buy ready-made meals. Take homemade snacks (e.g., sandwiches) outside, instead of buying them.
- Look for items in charity shops or second-hand shops.
- Look out for goods that are on sale. Big sales in the UK are in the spring, autumn and after Christmas.
- Scan university notice boards for second-hand books sold by other students. Books can also be borrowed from the library.
- Think about your attitude towards spending money. Your spending priorities may change when you are a student. Decide whether you really need expensive items.

Bringing and transferring money to the UK

It is advisable not to bring a large amount of cash to the UK; there is a risk it could get lost or stolen. Further, certain countries limit the amount of money that can be taken out. A safer alternative is to bring enough money to cover your immediate needs on arrival and for the first few weeks, and to transfer the rest of the money that you need. There are several ways to send money to the UK:

- travellers' cheques or travellers cheque card
- International Money Order (IMO) or bank draft (issued by a bank in your country and deposited into a British bank).
- telegraphic money transfer
- electronic transfer
- a cheque (drawn in sterling on a UK bank) in your country
- cash transfer.

Each method has advantages and disadvantages; for example, certain methods are securer or quicker, or cheaper. Ask your bank in your country for advice on the best method to use. Your university will have a preference about how their accommodation and tuition fees should be paid.

Foreign currency and travellers' cheques can be changed at banks and building societies, post offices, travel agents, tourist information offices, and Bureaux de Change offices. Airports, ports, and larger train stations often have places to change money. There is likely to be a charge to change money, such as commission (a percentage of the amount you exchange) and, sometimes, a handling fee.

Make a note of the exchange rates because they determine how much pound sterling you can get from your currency. Compare the rate at different places. Exchange rates can also vary daily.

Note that it is easier for some students to bring and exchange US dollars or other currencies instead of their own country's currency.

Banks and bank accounts

Open a bank account as soon as you arrive. Major banks include:

- Abbey
- Barclays
- Co-operative
- Halifax
- HSBC
- Lloyds TSB
- NatWest
- Royal Bank of Scotland.

Building societies and Post Offices also offer accounts. Types of accounts include:

- *Current account*. Used for everyday withdrawals and deposits, and allows the use of a debit card or a cheque to pay for goods.
- *Deposit/investment account*. A savings account that offers a high rate of interest but offers fewer services and has restrictions about how money can be accessed. Suitable for large sums of money rather than for everyday finances.
- *Internet account*. All or most transactions take place online. Provides easy tracking of account details, but you might not be able to visit a bank in person.

Unfortunately, the types of accounts available to international students are limited. However, some banks offer special accounts for international students with a range of services.

Opening an account

To open an account, you will need to visit a bank, fill in application forms and perhaps attend an interview. You will be asked for your personal details as well as several of the following items to confirm your identity, student status, and address:

- ID card
- passport
- cash (as a first deposit)
- a letter from your university confirming that you are a student
- a letter from your family or sponsor confirming that you have enough funding
- a document confirming your address
- information about your bank account at home.

Check with the bank to find out what documents they require.

Different banks and accounts offer different facilities. There are several factors to consider:

- location of the bank (on campus or near the university)
- opening times of the bank
- facilities and services the bank can offer you, such as a bank card and cheque book, use of other banks' cash machines, and direct debits and standing orders
- services and costs for transferring money from your country
- internet banking
- whether the account operates in accordance with Sharia principles
- bank charges, which can sometimes be high (e.g., for unauthorised overdrafts).

It can be difficult for students on short courses (less than a year) to open an account. They will need to make alternative arrangements to manage their finances (e.g., using travellers cheques or bank cards issued outside the UK).

Depositing and withdrawing money

A convenient way to withdraw money is to use a cash card at a cash machine (ATM). Cash machines are located inside and outside banks, as well as in public places, such as in shopping centres or outside supermarkets. There is usually no fee to withdraw money from a cash machine, although certain machines charge a fee (e.g., if you use one at another bank). Cash can also be taken out from a bank by completing a form and handing it to the cashier. Another way to obtain money is to ask for 'cash back' when you use your card at a supermarket to pay for your shopping; this means that the cashier will give you cash, which is then taken from your account at the same time you pay for your shopping.

To put cash or cheques into your account, fill in a form at the bank and give it to a cashier along with the money. Cash will go into your account on the same day it is deposited, but it takes several working days for a cheque to clear.

How to pay for goods

As well as using cash, there are other ways to pay for goods and services:

- *Debit card* (e.g., Switch, Delta or Solo). This is a plastic card that can be used to pay for goods (the money is transferred directly from your bank account to the shop).
- *Credit card* (e.g., Visa or MasterCard). To buy things without paying for them immediately. The money can be paid back to the credit card company in instalments, and interest is charged on the money borrowed. Credit cards are usually only issued to people with a regular income. An alternative is to obtain a card from your country and use it in the UK.
- *Cheque*. A cheque can also be used to pay for items. You will need to show a 'cheque guarantee card', which guarantees that the bank will pay, up to a limit, the cheque that you write. Shops do not always accept cheques for small amounts.
- *Direct debit/standing order*. Some companies prefer to collect regular payments (e.g., rent and bills) from a customer's bank account. This is a common way to pay rent and utility bills.

Some cards function as a combined cash, debit, and cheque guarantee card. When you use a bank card you will be asked to enter your Personal Identification Number (PIN) on a keypad, also known as 'Chip and Pin'.

Finding a part-time job during your studies

Working part-time during term-time is a good way to earn extra money, obtain work experience, and meet new people. If chosen carefully, work experience can fill gaps in your skills and knowledge, and help you to gain an insight into careers that interest you. However, a job can be time-consuming – think carefully about how much time you can spare. Balancing a job with your studies can be very challenging.

Employment restrictions

In order to study in the UK, most international students must show that they have sufficient funds to cover their expenses without working. However, you may be allowed to work part-time. There are different immigration rules for EEA nationals, who are generally allowed to work without restrictions, and non-EEA nationals who may have restrictions. Check the immigration conditions and UK employment regulations that apply to you. You can contact the Home Office (Border and Immigration Agency) for advice. You can also look at the visa or other documents in your passport. There may be restrictions about the number of hours and type of work you are authorised to do.

In addition to immigration conditions, universities might have restrictions to ensure that your academic work is not affected.

If you are not allowed to work, but want to, you should seek advice from your university's international support office. Never work illegally or more than the permitted number of hours; otherwise, you could be fined, your visa could be cancelled, or you could be sent back to your own country (deported)!

Typical jobs for students

Jobs available to students are mainly in the hospitality, retail, and service sectors in cafes, bars, restaurants, shops, supermarkets, and call centres. Typical part-time jobs include waiter/waitress, shop assistant, bartender, cleaner, and office assistant.

Other options include an internship (a supervised work placement in a company, often during the summer vacation or during a semester) and a sandwich course (a period of employment that is part of a degree course).

The hours and rates of pay vary. Students typically work on weekends and evenings so that their job does not clash with classes. Expect to earn about £7 per hour. The law states that employers must pay a minimum amount per hour (called the national minimum wage). Most employers pay wages into your bank account, although a few pay cash in hand.

Where to look for a job

Universities have a job shop that helps students to find part-time work, and a careers advice centre that gives guidance on how to apply for jobs and prepare for interviews. Other places to look for jobs include adverts in local job centres, newspapers, shops, restaurant windows, and university notice boards. Ask other students how they found their job and if they know of any vacancies. Chapter 10 explains how to search and apply for jobs.

Income Tax and National Insurance

Tax must be paid on any money earned in the UK. There are two main types of tax – Income Tax and National Insurance. They will be deducted from your wages by your employer, and you should be given a pay slip that shows your Income Tax and National Insurance contributions. The amount of tax you need to pay depends on your salary. Not all of your income is taxable – you only pay tax if you earn above a certain level (around £5,000), known as your personal tax allowance. If you will not earn more than your personal tax allowance, you can arrange for tax not to be deducted from your salary. More information about UK tax is available from HM Revenue and Customs.

When you are actively seeking work or start work, you will need a National Insurance number, which is issued by the UK government to ensure that National Insurance contributions are recorded. The number should only be used by you. Applications for a National Insurance number can be made at a local Department for Work and Pensions office (e.g., a local Jobcentre). They will need to see identification, details of the job (a letter from your employer confirming that you have been offered work), and evidence that you are entitled to work. Further information is available from your local Jobcentre.

5 Daily life and culture in the UK

INTRODUCTION

After reading this chapter, you should:

- ☑ Know about the UK's geography and climate
- ☑ Understand British customs, manners, and etiquette.
- ☑ Be prepared for daily life such as eating out and shopping
- ☑ Consider extra arrangements and support for your family

This chapter introduces the UK and its people, geography, climate, customs, and governance. There are details about daily life, including British food and drink, shopping, using public transport, and socialising. There is also an overview of the arrangements and support to consider if your family will accompany you to the UK.

Introduction to the UK

People in different countries use a variety of names to refer to the UK, such as Britain, the British Isles, or England. However, the official name is the 'United Kingdom of Great Britain and Northern Ireland', which is commonly abbreviated to the 'UK'. The UK is located in northwest Europe, and consists of a large island called Great Britain, a region known as Northern Ireland, many small islands, and overseas territories. The country is separated from the rest of Europe by the English Channel in the south and the North Sea in the east. There is a channel tunnel that connects England to France via a train called the Eurostar.

Characteristics of the UK

Population	60.6 million; third largest country in Europe
Area	244,820 sq km
Climate	Generally mild and temperate. Cool summers and fairly mild winters.
Languages	English is the dominant and official language. Welsh is common in parts of Wales; Scottish Gaelic is spoken in areas in Scotland; and Irish Gaelic in some places in Northern Ireland. Ethnic groups also use other languages.
Religion	Christianity is the most common religion. Other prominent religions include Islam, Sikhism, Judaism, Hinduism, and Buddhism.
Major cities	The capital city is London. Other major cities include Birmingham, Manchester, Sheffield, Liverpool, Bristol, and Nottingham. In Scotland, the capital city is Edinburgh, and the largest city is Glasgow. The capital city of Wales is Cardiff, and the capital city of Northern Ireland is Belfast.
Highest mountain	Ben Nevis (1,343 metres), located in Scotland.
Longest river	The Severn.
Largest lake	Loch Morar (310 metres deep), located in Scotland.

Regions

Great Britain consists of three regions: England, Scotland, and Wales. Northern Ireland is located to the north east of the Republic of Ireland. The largest and most populous region is England. It consists mostly of a lowland landscape, particularly in the south and south west; mountainous terrain and limestone hills in the north; and chalk hills in the south. The highest mountain in England is Scafell Pike, located in the Lake District National Park. The main rivers and estuaries include the Severn, Thames, Trent, Tyne, and Humber.

   Scotland is located in the north, and it is the second largest and most populous region. It's capital city is Edinburgh. There are rural highlands in the north and west, uplands in the south and east, and many offshore islands, including two large groups of islands known as the Orkney and Shetland islands. Scotland has many mountains, lakes, firths and lochs. The largest rivers are the Tey, Spey, and Clyde. Some people in Scotland speak a language called Gaelic.

Wales is located in the west, and it is generally mountainous, particularly in the north and central areas. The majority of the population, and the capital city Cardiff, is located in the south. Other big cities include Swansea and Newport. The highest mountain is Snowdon, located in Snowdonia. There are many waterfalls, including Pistyll Rhaeadr in Powys. About 20 per cent of the population speak a language called Welsh. The national game of Wales is rugby.

Northern Ireland is mostly mountainous, and has many drumlins (small hills). There are uplands and lowlands, such as the uplands of County Antrim in the north east. The main river is the Shannon. There is Lough Neagh, the largest lake in the UK, and Lough Erne, which is a lake and network of islands. The capital city of Northern Ireland is Belfast.

Population

More than 60.6 million people live in the UK, mostly in major cities. The population is predominantly made up of the English, Scottish, Welsh, Irish, and immigrants who live and work in the country. People move around the four regions of the UK more than they used to, but there are regional differences, such as accent and traditions. For example, many people in England, Scotland, Northern Ireland, and Wales speak English using a regional dialect, which includes a different pronunciation, and unique words and grammar.

The UK welcomes and celebrates cultural diversity. British society is ethnically diverse, and there is a wide range of cultural, racial, and religious backgrounds. The main ethnic groups are Black African and Caribbean, Bangladeshi, Chinese, Indian, and Pakistani. There are also significant numbers from Australia, Canada, Italy, Poland, and the USA. There are equal opportunities in areas such as education, employment, and health care, and there are laws to protect people from discrimination.

Climate

The climate is generally mild and temperate, with cool summers and fairly mild winters. There are four seasons: winter (December to February), spring (March to May), summer (June to August), and autumn (September to November). The weather is changeable, and can vary widely from day-to-day. Temperatures rarely fall below -10°C (14°F), or rise above 32°C (90°F). There is abundant rainfall throughout the year, although autumn and winter are the wettest seasons. There

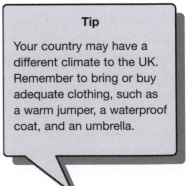

Tip

Your country may have a different climate to the UK. Remember to bring or buy adequate clothing, such as a warm jumper, a waterproof coat, and an umbrella.

is snowfall in some areas during winter and spring. In recent years there have been summer heat waves.

The UK consists of England, Scotland, and Wales (Great Britain) and Northern Ireland.

The weather also depends on the location. In general, the east is drier than the west, and the south is the warmest. The weather tends to be more extreme in mountainous hilly areas; for example, there tends to be more snow in Scotland than in the south.

Government, politics, and law

The UK is a parliamentary democracy, which means that parliament makes legalisation. Parliament consists of elected representatives (known as Members of Parliament, or MPs), the House of Lords (in which non-elected members propose, amend, and revise legislation), and the Queen.

MPs belong to different political parties. The largest political parties are the Labour Party, Conservative Party, and Liberal Democrats. The party with the majority of support forms the government, and its leader, known as the Prime Minister, is the head of the government. MPs meet in a room called the House of Commons, where they discuss legislation. A group of senior ministers, known as the Cabinet, make important policy decisions and head departments. The second largest political party forms the Opposition party that challenges government decisions and suggests alternatives. The Opposition also has a leader and a shadow cabinet.

The UK government is a constitutional monarchy, which means that the Queen is the head of state. Her duties include opening parliament, closing parliament before a general election, and approving legislation.

Although parliament makes legalisation, a number of issues are decided at the regional level, in the Scottish Parliament, National Assembly for Wales or, when it is sitting, the Northern Ireland Assembly. They are responsible for regional issues, including development, education, health, and social services. For more information about the UK government, visit the Houses of Parliament website.

The UK is a member of the European Union (EU), which is a confederation of different countries. The countries pool some of their sovereignty to work together on economic, judicial and security issues. The EU proposes and passes laws which also become law in the UK.

Economy and money

The UK is a leading financial and trading centre, and has one of the world's largest economies. The economy is stable, and is experiencing continuous growth and low inflation. It is a free market, and based primarily on private enterprise; many state-owned enterprises have been privatised since the 1980s. The currency is pound sterling, represented by the symbol £.

The UK was the first country to experience the industrial revolution. The economy focused initially on heavy industry and manufacturing. However, heavy industry has declined throughout the 20th century, and is being replaced by the service sector. Financial services, business services, and insurance companies now dominate the economy. Tourism and agriculture play an important role. Although heavy industry is declining, they are still important, especially coal, oil, and agriculture. Creative industries – such as advertising and television production – are also significant.

Royal Family

The UK has a royal family that dates back over ten centuries. Queen Elizabeth II has been on the throne since 1952. She is married to Prince Phillip (the Duke of

Edinburgh), who is the son of Prince and Princess Andrew of Greece and Denmark. The Queen has three children, including Prince Charles (The Prince of Wales), who is the heir to the throne. Prince Charles has two sons – Princes William and Harry. Other members of the Royal Family include the Queen's other children, grandchildren, cousins, and their spouses. The Queen lives in Buckingham Palace in London, and in other residences such as Windsor Castle in England, and Balmoral Castle and Holyroodhouse Palace in Scotland.

The Queen and the Royal Family play an important role, and participate in ceremonial roles, public duties, and charity work. The Queen also approves legislation passed by parliament, and acts as the Head of the Church of England and the Armed Services. There are many royal traditions, such as 'Changing the Guard' at Buckingham Palace, in which new guards change duty. To learn more about the Royal Family and royal traditions, visit the Buckingham Palace website.

British food and drink

There is a wide range of cuisine to choose from. There are traditional dishes, as well as many foods from around the world. Traditional British dishes include fish and chips, English breakfast, roast dinners, Yorkshire pudding, and afternoon tea. Although traditional dishes remain popular, nowadays many foods from around the world are commonly available. Popular ethnic cuisine includes Chinese, French, Greek, Indian, Italian, and Thai.

Meals

People eat three or four meals a day; breakfast, lunch, dinner, and sometimes supper. Breakfast cereal, or toast with marmalade or butter, is commonly eaten for breakfast. A traditional English breakfast is made up of bacon, egg, sausage, mushroom, and tomatoes. A range of dishes is eaten for lunch and dinner. Main meals are often followed with a sweet dessert.

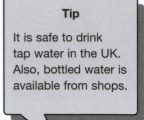

Tip

It is safe to drink tap water in the UK. Also, bottled water is available from shops.

Popular drinks include tea and coffee (served with or without milk), herbal teas, fruit juices, and soft drinks. In addition to small meals, snacks such as sandwiches, biscuits, chocolate, and crisps are popular.

It is traditional for a family to eat together for Sunday dinner, which includes beef, roast potatoes, brussel sprouts, Yorkshire pudding, and gravy.

Food ingredients

Ingredients for cooking are widely available from local shops and supermarkets. Shops sell fresh food, as well as ready-made meals in tins and plastic containers that can be warmed by microwave oven. Organic food (food produced without use of synthetic fertilisers or pesticides) is increasing in popularity, although it is more expensive. An increasing number of people are vegetarian, which means that they only eat vegetables and vegetable products. Vegetarian food is widely available in supermarkets and restaurants.

Many foods are labelled with nutritional contents, including the number of calories they contain, and whether they are suitable for vegetarians.

Eating out

You will be spoilt for choice when eating out. The university campus and nearby areas have many places to dine. They include cafes (which serve tea and coffee, and small dishes), pubs (which sell alcohol and basic dishes), fast food outlets, and restaurants. Traditional British take-away food includes fish and chips, sausage in batter, steak and kidney pie, and mushy peas. Other popular take-away includes pizza, American-style fast food, Chinese meals, kebabs, and ethnic dishes. Opening hours of food outlets vary, and generally open at meal times and late at night. Many offer a delivery service and charge extra for it.

Traditional British dishes

Main meal	
Fish and chips	Fish that is deep-fried in batter, served with chips that are sprinkled with salt and malt vinegar.
English breakfast	A substantial breakfast that includes bacon, baked beans, eggs, fried bread, mushrooms, and tomatoes (it can also include other dishes). Often served with tea and coffee. In Scotland, the traditional breakfast may include lorne slices (sausage) and Ayrshire bacon.
Hot pot	A meat and vegetable stew that is cooked slowly in the oven.
Shephard's Pie	A pie that consists of lamb and vegetables, and is topped with mash potato. Cottage pie uses minced beef instead of lamb.
Toad in the hole	Roasted sausages covered in batter.
Yorkshire pudding	A savoury dish made from baked batter. Often served with roast beef and gravy.
Sausage and mash	Good quality sausages served with mashed potato and onion gravy.

(Continued)

Bubble and squeak	Chopped vegetables (usually cabbage and mashed potato) that are shaped into patties and fried.
Ploughman's Lunch	A cold meal or snack. Includes a thick slice of cheese, crusty fresh bread, pickle, pickled onions, and sometimes a salad.
Afternoon tea	Tea or coffee that is served with a snack, such as sandwiches, cream scones, or assorted pastries. Served at 4 o'clock.
Desserts	
Rhubarb crumble	Baked rhubarb topped with crumble (a mixture of sugar, flour, and butter). Served with custard or cream.
Trifle	A cake that includes fruit, sponge, jelly, and custard. Ingredients are arranged in layers, with sponge at the bottom, and cream and fruit at the top.
Bread and butter pudding	Baked buttered bread slices and raisins.
Spotted dick	Steamed pudding with dried fruit (sultanas and raisins).
Strawberries and cream	Fresh strawberries served with whipped cream.

There are regional variations in traditional food. For example, in Scotland the national dish is Haggis, and game (wild animals hunted for food) and salmon are popular. In Wales, traditional foods include laver bread (seaweed rolled in oatmeal and fried), Welsh Rarebit (melted cheese on toast), leeks, and Welsh cakes. Traditional food in Northern Ireland includes the Ulster fry, which consists of fried bacon, eggs, sausage, mushrooms, soda bread, and potato farl.

Manners and etiquette

Every country has social rules about correct and polite behaviour. Good manners show politeness, appreciation, and give a good impression. Below are examples of good manners and social skills in the UK.

- *Greetings*. It is usual to say 'Hello' or 'Good morning/afternoon/evening' when greeting people. More formal greetings include a handshake and 'How do you do?' or 'Nice to meet you'. People use the first name to greet people informally, and the title (Mr, Mrs, Miss, Dr, etc) with the surname formally. Cheek kissing as a social gesture is not as common as in other European countries, but it is an acceptable greeting for two friends and family members of the opposite gender to greet each other in this way.

- *Timing*. Be punctual! It is generally polite to arrive on time, and rude to be late. Arrange a time in advance before visiting someone, as it is impolite to turn up unexpected. It is a good idea to inform others in advance if you are going to be late.
- *Queuing*. Queuing is very common. It is bad mannered to jump a queue!
- *Smoking*. Smoking is not allowed in university buildings, in public buildings, on public transport, and sometimes in other people's homes.
- *Listening*. Be willing to listen to others. Try not to make assumptions about what other people are thinking about.
- *Tipping*. It is common in restaurants to leave extra money for the service (known as a 'tip'), usually 10–15 per cent of the bill. Some restaurants include the tip in the bill as a 'service charge'. A tip is not needed in a fast food restaurant.

Table Manners

Most food is eaten with cutlery (a knife, fork, and spoon). When you have finished eating, the knife and fork should be placed together.

- To show your appreciation, say thank you when food is served. If you eat at a friend's home, or as a guest in a restaurant, it is polite to say that the food is delicious (even if it is not).
- Begin eating only after everyone has been served and your host has started.
- Do not eat food too fast, and try not to finish before your companions.
- It is inappropriate to ask to take left-over food home.
- Do not play with food and try not to smoke when dining.
- Try not to cough, sneeze, or burp at the table. If you must, do so away from the table, and cover your nose with a napkin.
- Sit up straight, and do not rest elbows on the table while eating.
- It is rude to open your mouth, talk, spit, or make loud noises when eating.
- Do not use your fingers to remove food from your teeth.
- Ask someone to pass items to you if you cannot reach it easily.
- Napkins should be unfolded and put on your lap.
- Consider switching off your mobile phone as it could disturb others.

Entertainment

There are ample social and recreational activities. There is something for everyone. You can live your life as quietly or actively as you want to!

Popular entertainment among students includes drinking alcoholic and non-alcoholic beverages in pubs and bars; dancing in nightclubs; watching movies in cinemas;

attending music events; and socialising in cafes. There are many cultural activities such as theatre and musicals, museums, art galleries, classical music concerts, ballet, and opera. The Student Union is the hub of student social life. It organises social activities on and off campus. Clubs and societies at your university organise social activities. Events that are organised by universities tend to be cheaper than similar events outside. Further information about entertainment events is available from your Student Union, student and local newspapers, and local library. Look out for posters around campus.

Making friends

Making friends in a different country and culture is not as difficult as it seems. There are many opportunities to do so.

- To make conversation, ask people about their course, hobbies, etc. Try to use open-ended questions (questions that cannot be answered with a yes or no answer). Always be polite and respectful to others.
- Do not worry too much about your English language ability. It is not necessary to have perfect pronunciation and grammar to be understood. If you don't understand others, ask them to speak slower or to explain it differently.
- It is easier to make friends if you participate in social activities and excursions organised by your university, including social events for international students.
- Go to the Student Union's bar, coffee bar, and other places to meet people.
- Consider activities such as attending church or helping with voluntary work.
- Keep in contact with people who you meet.
- If you want to travel on holiday, ask a travel agent about the possibility of joining a tour group.

Getting around – public transport

There is a comprehensive public transport system which can be used to reach most locations in the country. Services include bus, coach, rail, taxi, and, for longer distances, air services. Public transport is generally reliable, safe, and comfortable.

Bus and coach

It is convenient and cheap to travel by bus. Timetables are available at bus stops, and bus company offices and their websites.

Longer distances can be travelled via coach, which link most cites and towns. The main coach operators include National Express and Scottish Citylink.

Coach tickets are cheaper than train tickets. You can save 30 per cent off National Express coach travel by purchasing a Young Persons Coachcard, which is available for full-time students and young people aged between 16 and 26.

How to catch a bus

Catching a bus in the UK might differ from your country.

- Queue at the bus stop, and wait your turn to board.
- The route number and destination are displayed on the front of the bus.
- Put your hand out to signal for an approaching bus to stop.
- It is polite to allow passengers to leave the bus before you alight.
- Inform the driver where you are going, and pay the fare. Try to give the driver the correct fare because they may not be able to issue change.
- Buy a single or return ticket. It is possible to buy a bus pass that can be used for a longer time, such as for a week or month.
- When you approach your destination, press the bell to signal the driver to stop.

Rail

Major train stations are located in large cities, and many town centres have smaller stations. Tickets should be purchased in advance at ticket offices, self-service machines in train stations, via telephone from National Rail Enquiries, or at certain travel agents. It may be possible to buy tickets on the train if a station does not sell them.

A train ticket can be expensive, especially for longer distances; the fare depends on the distance you travel and when you buy the ticket. There is usually a discount if it is bought in advance, if you use a discount card, or if you travel outside peak times. A cheaper ticket, however, generally has more restrictions concerning when it can be used.

There are different types of train tickets. Some are flexible and allow travel on any train at any time, whereas others are restricted to certain times or trains. The main types of tickets are:

- *Standard open and Standard day tickets.* Valid on the date shown on the ticket, and can be used at any time of the day.
- *Cheap day tickets.* Valid on the date shown on the ticket, and are limited to off-peak times.
- *Saver and super-saver tickets*. Cheaper and have more limitations, such as off-peak travel only.
- *Super advance and Apex tickets.* Booked in advance, and are cheaper, but are restricted to selected routes and the date shown on the ticket.

Information about train services and timetables is available from National Rail Enquiries, The Trainline, and Traveline.

Young Persons Railcard

People aged 16–25 (or aged 26 or over and in full-time education) can buy a Young Persons Railcard to receive up to 30 per cent off the price of certain types of tickets. To obtain a railcard, fill in an application form at a train station, and provide identification, photographs, and a fee. You will also need to show proof that you are a full-time student. If your application is successful, you will be issued with a railcard. The application form is available from a staffed ticket office, or online at www.railcards-online.co.uk

---

The London Underground

At first glance the London Underground (also known as 'the tube') may seem daunting. However, it is easy and convenient to use.

Planning your journey
Look at a map of the Underground to plan your journey. Maps are available at most stations and on trains. There are 12 train lines, and each one has a different name and is represented

by a different colour on the map. For example, the Northern Line, which runs from north to south London, is coloured black, whereas the Central Line, which runs from east to west, is red. Find the line you will start on and the station you are going to, and then see how many lines and zones you need to travel in to reach your destination.

Buying a ticket

Tickets are available from ticket offices or self-service machines at stations. It is quicker to use a machine; they should give change and also accept credit and debit cards. The price of the ticket depends on the zone you start and finish in (the Underground is divided into 6 zones; the city centre is Zone 1), and whether it is a single or return.

If you use the underground regularly you can buy travel cards for daily, weekly and monthly travel. They can also be used on some buses and railways services in the London area. Alternatively, you can buy an 'Oyster card', which is a plastic card that can be swiped across a card reader at the turnstile (it is often cheaper to use it instead of buying tickets).

Entering and leaving the station

To enter and leave a station you will need to pass through a turnstile. It opens when you put your ticket, with the black magnetic strip facing downwards, into a slot in the turnstile, and reappears when you pass through. Remember to collect your ticket after you pass through; if the ticket is for a single journey, it will stay in the machine when you leave the station). There are colour-coded directions to help you reach the line you want.

On the train

When a train arrives at the station, the doors should open automatically, or you may need to press the illuminated 'open' button. If you make a mistake and go in the wrong direction, don't worry; you can get off at the next stop and change to the opposite platform. There are also station attendants to give advice.

The Underground generally opens at 5.30am and closes around midnight. There is a limited service on Sundays. It is better to avoid busy rush hours (8am–9.30am and 4pm–6pm) and travelling alone at night. For more information about the London Underground, contact Travel Information Centres at several London train stations, Transport for London (www.tfl.gov.uk), and the London Underground website (www.thetube.com).

Taxis

Taxis can be expensive. It is customary to book a taxi via telephone, although traditional London taxis can be hailed in the street. Telephone numbers of taxi companies can be found in the telephone directory, or on university notice boards. Only use taxis that are registered with the local authority, and ask for the price of the journey before you depart, especially if there is no meter in the taxi. Taxi companies often give discounts to students.

Bicycle

A cheaper and quicker alternative is to use a bicycle to travel around your area. It is generally safe to cycle in the UK, although there are difficulties in certain places due to poor roads, heavy traffic, hilly terrain, and bad weather. A new bicycle can be bought from a bike shop; a cheaper option is to look for a second-hand one in local newspaper advertisements or university notice boards. There is the National Cycle Network, which is a set of cycle routes across the UK. For more about cycling in London, including route maps, visit the London Cycling Campaign website (www.lcc.org.uk).

Safety while cycling

- Be familiar with your route and look for cycle signs.
- Keep your bicycle in good working order. Regularly check the brakes, chain, and wheels.
- Use lights, and fluorescent/reflective clothing when riding at night.
- Wear a cycle helmet.
- Be aware of cars and pedestrians around you. Use mirrors to view traffic behind.
- Learn about the Highway Code. It is a set of rules that apply to all road users. More is available from www.highwaycode.gov.uk
- Always lock your bicycle when not in use.

Travelling by plane

The UK has a range of airports and airlines, including budget airlines that offer low prices. It is advisable to book as early as possible to obtain the best fare. Popular airlines include:

- British Airways
- BMI
- Bmibaby
- Ryanair
- EasyJet
- Flybe.

Owning and driving a car

The law and procedures for driving in the UK may be very different to those in your country. Before driving you must ensure that you meet all of the legal requirements that apply to you and your vehicle. For example, you will need to be over a certain age, have a valid driving licence, insurance, road tax, and proof that your vehicle is roadworthy. If you have a licence that was issued in your country, you may be able to use it in the

UK. Students from EEA countries are generally able to drive while their licence is valid, or exchange it for a British one. Some students from other countries may be allowed to use a valid licence issued in their country for a certain time period, and then apply for a UK driving licence. Check the legal requirements before you drive. For up-to-date information about the rules and regulations, contact the DVLA in England, Wales, and Scotland, and the DVLNI in Northern Ireland.

If you don't have a valid licence, you can learn to drive. Lessons are available from driving schools and approved instructors (look in your local telephone directory for their details). Before learning, you will need to apply for a provisional licence; applications can be made at your local Post Office. You are not allowed to drive on your own until you pass the driving test.

There are various motoring organisations you can join that provide services such as breakdown and recovery services and advise about owning and driving a car. They include the AA and the RAC.

A list of car hire companies is available in a phone directory. National companies include Hertz, Thrifty Car Rental, and the National Car Rental.

Shopping

Everyday items such as food and household goods can be bought from local shops, newsagents, and supermarkets. The university campus will have shops.

The high street is the focal point of shopping and most national chain stores are located there. Big cities such as London, Cardiff, Birmingham, Manchester, and Edinburgh attract shoppers from around the world. There are also shopping centres on the outskirts of towns and cities that offer shops, restaurants, cinemas, and sports facilities.

Tip

Keep receipts for goods that you buy. You may need them if you want to return faulty or unsatisfactory goods.

Department stores are large retail stores that sell goods such as clothes, household items, electrical appliances, furniture and furnishings, and gifts. Major department stores include:

- Primark
- Debenhams
- Harrods
- John Lewis
- Marks and Spencer
- Selfridges
- Woolworths.

Supermarkets are large food stores located in towns and cities. Large supermarkets sell household goods, computers, mobile phones, and even financial services. Major supermarkets include:

- Asda
- Safeway
- Sainsbury's

- Marks and Spencer
- Tesco
- Waitrose.

Street markets sell goods from farmers and local producers, including fresh food, clothes, and shoes. Their goods are often cheaper than supermarkets. Famous markets in London include:

- Camden Market
- Spitalfields
- Portobello Road Market
- Berwick Street Market
- Greenwich Market.

Newsagents are smaller shops that sell newspapers, magazines, stationary, and snacks.

Other shops include bakers and patisseries, booksellers, charity shops, chemists, electrical goods shops, florists, gift shops, health shops, off-licences, pet shops, and petrol stations.

Opening hours are from 9am to 5pm (and a shorter time on Sundays). Shops, such as supermarkets, are open until the evening, and a few are open 24 hours a day. Internet shopping is increasing in popularity.

In recent years there has been increased awareness of ethical issues among shoppers. More and more people are buying products from companies that ensure that producers receive a good deal for their goods. Supermarkets sell Fair Trade products.

Buying and washing clothes

Clothes can be bought from department stores or clothes shops. Cheaper clothes are available in supermarkets or in charity shops. Bear in mind, however, that British clothes and shoe sizes could differ from your country.

Major clothes shops include:

- Gap
- House of Frazer
- Next
- Oasis

- River Island
- Topman
- Topshop.

University accommodation such as a hall of residence should have washing machines for their students. If not, you can wash your clothes in a launderette, which is a shop that has self-service coin-operated washing machines and dryers.

Practicing your religion

A range of religious faiths is represented in the UK and on the university campus. The most common faith is Christianity (the UK is a Christian country), and the second is Islam. Most Christians are members of the Church of England, or the Catholic Church (Roman Catholics); there are also other denominations nationwide. Other prominent religions in the country include Sikhism, Judaism, Hinduism, and Buddhism.

Everyone in the UK has the right to practise their faith. There are many opportunities to follow your religion and to be part of a religious community. Your options include:

- *The university chaplaincy*. A service that offers advice and support to students of all faiths and provides information about religious groups on campus. They also help to arrange religious services.
- *Student societies*. University societies and clubs where people of the same faith meet.
- Places of worship in the local area. All towns and cities have churches, mosques, synagogues, and prayer rooms.

Note that a large proportion of people do not have a religious affiliation, and church attendance is generally declining. Even so, people who do not regularly attend church do participate in religious ceremonies for births, marriages, and deaths.

Bringing your family to the UK

In normal circumstances it is possible for your spouse and children to stay with you in the UK while you are a student. You will need to consider the financial implications, as well as support for your family.

Immigration rules and employment

Immigration rules change regularly, and you should consult up-to-date information. There are different immigration rules for EEA nationals and non-EEA nationals. Generally, EEA nationals should be able to accompany you to the UK with no or few restrictions whereas non-EEA nationals will need to apply for permission, and will need to meet certain immigration criteria. For example, you may need to provide evidence that you and your spouses are married or in a civil partnership, and that you can financially support your family. There are also requirements for your child. Check the up-to-date regulations that are applicable.

Accommodation and finances

Universities have limited accommodation for families. Therefore, try to book it as early as you can, or ask to be put on the waiting list. Alternatively, you can look in the private sector for housing. If a suitable place to stay cannot be arranged before you leave your country, it might be easier and cheaper for you to arrive alone to find somewhere. In addition, bear in mind that accommodation arrangements may need to be booked first in order to satisfy your family's immigration regulations.

Living in the UK and supporting a family is expensive. Extra costs include family accommodation, childcare, and living costs. Be realistic about these extra costs. You and your spouse may be allowed to work, and you need to check if any restrictions exist. The stamp in your passport will also state whether or not employment is prohibited.

Childcare

Childcare for young children is expensive. The average price is about £120 per week, although state-run primary and secondary school is free. Childcare options for young children include a childminder, nursery, or playgroup. Your university should have a nursery on campus.

Further information about childcare options is available from the Childcare Link and the Daycare Trust, which are organisations that provide details of childcare providers.

Children older than 4 or 5 should attend school. Children aged between 4 and 11 attend primary school, whereas those between 11 and 16 attend secondary school. You have the option of sending them to a state-owned school, which is free, or a private (independent) school that charges fees. To obtain a place in a state school, contact the education department of the local government.

> **Tip**
>
> Ofstead is the official body for inspecting schools and childcare providers. You may wish to choose childcare providers that are registered with Ofstead.

School places are allocated according to where you live (called the 'Catchment Area'), though it may be possible to choose a school in another area. You can apply for a school place after you arrive in the UK, as it is necessary to have an address.

There are many factors to consider when choosing a school, such as its performance, how students are selected, whether the school is affiliated to a religion, and the travelling distance between school and home. Before you make a decision, it is advisable to visit the school, and to discuss your needs with the Head Teacher. Possible questions to ask are whether there are other international children at the school and the availability of support for children whose first language is not English. Do bear in mind, however, that your choice of school could be restricted if places are limited, especially if the school is not in your local area.

Performance data for different schools is available from:

- England: Department for Education and Skills
- Wales: National Assembly for Wales
- Scotland: HM Inspectorate of Education
- Northern Ireland: Department of Education.

The school year runs from September through to July. There are holidays at Christmas, and Easter, and one-week holidays in October, February, and May. Holidays roughly coincide with university holidays, but you might need to make child care arrangements in the school holidays or after school.

Children older than 16 can either continue with their education or take employment. Further education is usually not free.

Health and welfare

Think about how your family will adapt to the UK lifestyle and culture. It will be different to what they are used to, and they will not have access to the same advice, support, and facilities at university as you (because they will not be registered students at the university). Ask your university to see what support they can provide for your family.

6 Health, welfare, and safety

In this chapter there is information about the help and support that is available if you are ill or have personal problems. There are also tips to protect your belongings against crime, and advice about how to deal with discrimination.

Health care

Health care in the UK is provided by the National Health Service (NHS), which is a government-funded system. The NHS is divided into primary care (such as a local doctor, dentist, optician, etc.) and secondary care (hospitals). The NHS provides a wide range of health care services, which are summarised below. Private health care services are also available, but are expensive.

Doctor	Provides advice and diagnosis on a range of health problems. Conducts body examinations, gives treatment, issues prescriptions for medicine, and carries out simple surgical operations. A local doctor is known as a general practitioner (GP).
Hospitals	Deal with medical problems and procedures that cannot be done by a GP. This is the place to go for emergency treatment.
Dentist	Specialises in the care of the mouth, teeth, and gums. Conducts mouth examinations, offers treatment, and gives advice about oral health.

Pharmacist (Chemist)	Prepares and provides medicine. Gives advice about health, how to use medicine, and can offer testing for problems such as diabetes, allergies, and food intolerance.
Optician	Examines and tests the health of eyes. Prescribes and dispenses glasses.
Chiropodist	Assesses, diagnoses, and treats lower limb problems (feet and nails).
Psychologist	Helps patients overcome emotional and personal matters (e.g., anxiety, depression, relationship problems, etc).
Other services	There are a range of other services such as physiotherapy, maternity and child care, social services, speech and language therapy, and occupational therapists.

What can I do if I am ill?

You should dial 999 if someone is seriously ill or has a serious injury that requires immediate attention. However, the first step for most people seeking medical treatment is to visit their GP's office (known as a doctor's surgery) to see a doctor. You will need to make an appointment to see a GP. If the condition is not urgent, an appointment can take two working days or more. In an emergency, a doctor might be willing to visit your home if you are too ill to visit the surgery; requests for home visits need to be made as early in the day as possible (e.g., in the morning).

> **Tip**
>
> The NHS provides a telephone service that provides advice about health issues. It is called NHS Direct or NHS 24, in Scotland.

GPs are able to treat most health problems, but they can refer patients to a specialist doctor (consultant) in a hospital department. If you need to see a GP but their surgery is closed (for example, in the evening), there will be a telephone number you can call for help with medical problems that cannot wait until the next day.

You can also consult a pharmacist for common complaints such as colds and coughs.

Dial 999 for medical emergencies

If you or someone needs immediate medical help, dial 999 and ask for the ambulance service. Alternatively, ask someone to take you to the nearest hospital with an Accident & Emergency department (A&E). This option is only for people who are seriously ill or have a serious injury that requires immediate attention. For non-emergency problems, visit your GP (alternatively, some cities have NHS walk-in centres, and some hospitals have Minor Injuries Units).

Registering with a GP

It is necessary to register with a GP before seeking their advice. To register, you should visit the GP's surgery and ask to be added as an NHS patient. You will need to fill in forms and provide documents such as your passport, proof of address, and evidence that you are a student. An NHS Medical Card may be issued that provides details such as your name, NHS number, and the name and address of your doctor.

It is important to register as soon as you can, and to not wait until the first time you are ill. If a doctor does not accept new patients, then try another one. You can change your doctor at any time by taking your Medical Card to a new GP's surgery to register. A list of GP surgeries is available from:

- NHS
- NHS Direct
- Local Primary Care Trusts (also known as a Local Health Board in Wales, or Central Services Agency in Northern Ireland)
- Public libraries.
- If you are away from the university, you should be able to see a local GP in the area you are visiting.

University health centres

Many universities have a health centre that provides health services (usually GP services) to students, staff, and their families. Registration at a health centre takes place during the Introduction Week or Freshers' Fair, alongside enrolment for other university services. If your university does not have a health service, or if you prefer not to use it, you can register at a local GP's surgery instead. University centres, like other GP surgeries, offer some or all of the following services:

- advice, diagnosis, and treatment of medical problems
- prescriptions for medicine
- travel health advice and vaccinations
- contraceptive devices
- medical certificates
- minor surgery
- advice about how to give up smoking, and how to lose weight
- referrals to consultants
- dental care and counselling services.

Medicine

Medicine is available from pharmacy stores (also known as chemists). Certain medicines can only be obtained with a medical prescription, which is permission from a doctor for the pharmacist to issue medicine. A doctor will give you a prescription after meeting you, although a repeat prescription is usually obtainable without a consultation. There is a fee for each prescription medicine. Not all medicines require a prescription, and are known as 'over-the-counter' medicine. As well as issuing medicine, pharmacists can give advice about different types of medicine, how to treat common health problems, and can give advice about adopting a healthier lifestyle.

Seeing a dentist and optician

Dental care is widely available. Patients eligible for NHS treatment can pay a reduced fee to see a dentist. However, many people find it difficult to find a dentist who provides NHS treatment; instead, they pay for private treatment. If you want NHS dental treatment, you first need to find a dentist that offers it, and then ask if you can be accepted as a patient. You can search for a dentist on the NHS website, or by telephoning NHS Direct. Your university health service doctor might have special arrangements for dental services.

Opticians are also widely available and are often located on high streets and shopping centres. Most students need to pay for the cost of eye tests and a pair of glasses.

How much does health care cost?

Certain health care is free for everyone, such as some initial emergency treatment, and treatment of certain communicable diseases. Also, the UK has agreements with selected countries, particularly those in the EEA, to offer NHS treatment for their residents.

Most international students should qualify for NHS treatment, although eligibility varies according to the length of course, nationality, and whether students are resident in England, Scotland, or Wales. Your dependents (partner and children) resident in the UK may be entitled to NHS treatment. You should check whether you are entitled to treatment, and the conditions associated with it. Also make sure that you have adequate medical insurance, especially if you are not eligible for emergency treatment.

Free services for people entitled to NHS treatment include seeing a GP, and treatment in hospital. Students who are not eligible for NHS treatment need to pay a fee. An alternative to NHS treatment is private health care, but the cost can be very expensive.

> **Tip**
>
> If you cannot keep an appointment with a doctor, inform them as soon as you can. If you fail to do so, you may need to pay a cancellation fee.

Getting help with NHS charges

Further information about NHS costs (prescriptions, dental charges, and optical fees) is available from the Department of Health. They produce a leaflet (HC11) 'Help with health costs', available from their website (www.dh.gov.uk), a post office, hospital, or social security office. Advice is also available from GPs, dentists, pharmacists, and opticians. To make a claim, you will need to fill in a form.

University Counselling Service

Your university should have a free counselling service that offers help and advice about personal or academic concerns. Counsellors can talk with you about your problems to help you understand and focus on them more clearly and to help develop solutions. Counsellors can assist with personal problems such as:

- adjusting to a new culture
- homesickness
- study issues
- anxiety, stress, and depression
- relationships, and sexuality and gender concerns
- dealing with dilemmas
- suicidal thoughts and self-harm.

The number of counselling sessions needed depends on the problem. The counselling service will also have a range of self-help materials, such as leaflets and booklets.

University nightline and other sources of help

Many universities have a 'nightline'. It is a telephone service (and sometimes an email service) run by trained students that offers listening and support for other students. You can telephone the nightline to talk to someone in confidence about issues.

Additional help is available from university staff, including your personal tutor, Director of Studies, international student advisors, and the Student Union. There will be support organisations in your local area; their contact details are available in your local telephone directory.

Alcohol and drugs

Many people enjoy drinking alcohol. Socialising in bars or pubs is an accepted and important part of student life. However, it is important to be aware of the harmful effects of excessive drinking. Over-consumption of alcohol can lead to physical and psychological harm, and social problems.

It is illegal in the UK to use non licensed drugs, or to use licensed drugs without medical supervision. Such use is dangerous to health, and could lead to legal penalties by the police. Universities do not tolerate alcohol and drug misuse on their campus, and have strict penalties for offenders.

If you are concerned about your drinking, or use of other drugs, discuss the problem with your GP and university counselling service. Confidential advice is also available from national support groups such as Alcoholics Anonymous and the National Drugs helpline.

Anxiety and stress

Anxiety and stress are normal and natural reactions to life's pressures and challenges. They result in physical, emotional, and mental changes. A mild amount of stress can have benefits, but too much stress can cause physical and mental health problems.

Stress is a part of student life. Typical issues in university that can cause stress include:

- too much work
- assignments, exams and revision
- meeting deadlines
- leaving home, and arriving in a new country
- living with roommates
- pressure to succeed
- poor relationships with teachers

Many other situations in life can be stressful, such as financial problems, relationships, employment issues, bereavement, and personal injury.

Symptoms of stress include:

Physical symptoms

- headache
- pounding heartbeat
- excessive sweating
- rapid breathing
- sleeplessness
- anxiety
- back and neck pain
- fatigue
- insomnia
- weight loss or gain.

Emotional and mental changes

- loss of concentration
- confusion
- forgetfulness
- poor judgment
- disorganisation
- negative self-talk
- mood swings.

The first step to managing stress is to recognise its symptoms. If possible, try to avoid or reduce the cause of stress, and change the way you respond to challenging situations. The box below provides techniques you can use to manage and reduce the stress in your life. You should also consider visiting your GP or student counsellor for advice.

Managing stress

The way that you deal with life's challenges will influence your mental and physical health, and your academic success. Here are some things to do to reduce and manage stress.

Increase awareness
Understand stress, what causes it, and how your body responds. This will help you to identify stress.

Talk

It helps to talk with your friends, family, GP, or counsellor. Share your experiences with other international students.

Write

Some people find it helpful to express their feelings or problem by writing. One way to do this is to keep a 'learning journal' to record your feelings and thoughts during your course.

Take a break

Walk away from stressful situations. Take regular breaks from your work. For example, read a book, listen to music, or watch a movie. If possible, get away from the source of the stress. A few days rest, or a holiday, will help you to relax. Have some fun, and enjoy a laugh!

Keep healthy

A healthy lifestyle can help to reduce and prevent the effects of stress. Eat a healthy diet, get adequate sleep, and avoid excessive caffeine, alcohol, and smoking. Your university should have sports' clubs and facilities to help to relieve your stress.

Relaxation

Try and relax. Spend some time doing things you enjoy, such as:

- play soothing music
- watch a movie
- light aromatherapy candles
- have a hot bath (and add some essential oils!)
- take deep breaths
- do gentle stretching, and meditation.

(Continued)

Visualisation

Use your imagination to combat stress. To do this, find a quite place, close your eyes, and imagine a place or object that is pleasing. It could be a waterfall on a mountain, or a palm tree on a sun-soaked beach!

Positive thinking

Maintain a positive attitude towards your work. Learn to control worries. Also, put problems into perspective – is the situation really as bad as you think?

Manage your time

Deadlines and workloads can be stressful. Improve your time management skills, such as keeping a daily planner, and prioritising work.

Learn from the experience!

Change your behaviour and study habits to reduce stress in your life. Plan relaxation techniques into your weekly timetable!

Meningitis and septicaemia

Meningitis is a very dangerous disease that causes inflammation of the lining of the brain. Septicaemia is blood poisoning that occurs when meningitis-causing bacteria enter the blood stream. Meningitis and septicaemia are spread among people via droplets from the mouth and nose. Although both infections are rare, transmission occurs more readily when large numbers of people live in close proximity, such as students in a hall of residence. Therefore, you should be aware and vigilant of meningitis and septicaemia. You can also make an appointment with a doctor to be immunised against certain types of the disease. Symptoms of meningitis are flu-like, and include:

- dislike of bright lights
- severe headache
- nausea
- red/purple rash that does not disappear when pressed firmly
- neck stiffness
- disorientation or confusion
- loss of consciousness.

Be vigilant of the symptoms of meningitis and septicaemia because they are life-threatening diseases. If you are concerned, see a doctor immediately or go to the Accident and Emergency department in a hospital. Several national organisations can provide more information about meningitis, such as the National Meningitis Trust and the Meningitis Research Foundation.

Support for disabled students

Universities welcome applications from disabled students. They willingly provide advice and support so that disabled students can study effectively. Depending on the circumstances, the type of support might include:

- a personal learning support plan
- assignment extensions
- car parking
- special consideration (e.g., special examination arrangements)
- IT support
- assistance with note-taking
- course materials available in alternative formats.

A disability can be disclosed on the application form, during induction and/or by visiting the university's Disability Officer. However, you should discuss your needs before applying for a course to make sure that the university is able to provide the support you require. The university could ask the student to find funding for support, which can be expensive. If applicable, check with your sponsor to find out if any financial funding is available for expenses linked to disabilities.

Sexual health and sexually transmitted diseases

Attitudes in the UK towards sexual activity may differ from those in your country and culture. It is acceptable for students and their partners to be involved in sexual relationships. The decision to engage in sexual activity is a personal choice.

You should follow your own values. Do not feel pressured to have sex, or to follow the behaviour or attitudes of other students.

You are responsible for your sexual health. If you begin a sexual relationship, it is important to practice safe sex to avoid unintended pregnancy or sexually transmitted infections (STIs). Using contraception reduces the risk of unintended pregnancy and acquiring STIs. Some STIs can be treated, but others – such as HIV/AIDS – are life-threatening. Contraception and advice is available from your GP or Family Planning Clinic. Emergency contraception (taken after sexual intercourse to avoid pregnancy) is available from a GP or pharmacies. It is also important to protect yourself emotionally; only engage in sexual relationships that you are comfortable with, enjoy, and that are based on mutual respect and agreement.

Sexual orientation

Everyone has different feelings about the kinds of sexual relationships they want. In the UK, people can explore different sexualities without discrimination or prejudice. Student life is a period of independence, and a time when some people experiment with their sexuality. Some students realise that they are gay. The Student Union may have a support group – commonly known as a Lesbian, Gay, Bisexual, and Transgender (LGBT) society – that offers support and that arranges social events for gay and other students to make like-minded friends. If you are confused about your sexual orientation, try and discuss it with someone you trust, the LGBT society, or the university counselling service. There will also be other support services in the local area.

Mental health problems

It is common for students to experience emotional and psychological difficulties at some point during their time at university. The problem could be a pre-existing condition, or could arise while at university. Mental health issues range from temporary difficulties, such as anxiety, to diagnosed mental health such as depression, eating disorders, and addiction. Mental health problems are not stigmatised by health care workers and university staff, and a great deal of support is available. If you are suffering from a mental health issue, advice is available from your university counselling and health service or GP. You can also contact Mind, which is a charity that provides help on a range of mental health issues. It is a good idea to inform your university so that they can make reasonable adjustments to help you to participate and engage fully in their activities.

Dealing and coping with unfair discrimination

The UK welcomes international students and values the diversity that they bring. There are equal opportunities for everyone on campus, as well as in other areas such as employment. However, sometimes a student may experience unfair discrimination based on, for example, their nationality, age, gender, sexuality, religious beliefs, and disability. Everyone has a right to study without discrimination and unfairness. Although it is not easy to deal with discrimination, it is important to address the issue to ensure that it does not happen again.

- Make it clear to the person concerned that discrimination is not acceptable.
- Consider the situation carefully. Ask yourself if discrimination really did occur, or if there was a misunderstanding. Although some people hurt others deliberately, others unintentionally cause distress through thoughtlessness, or because they lack knowledge of other people's differences (e.g., culture).
- Seek support from your friends, family, the student's union, and the university's counselling service. You can also report the incident to your personal tutor.
- Decide whether to deal with the issue informally or formally. Informal action includes talking or writing to the person concerned (or asking a third party to do so) to explain that their actions are not acceptable. Formal action involves reporting and making an official complaint to the university, or taking legal action (there are laws to protect people from discrimination). If the behaviour is serious, you should report it to the police immediately.
- It is a good idea to collect evidence of the discrimination, especially if you intend to take formal action. Keep a written record of what happened, including the time, date, and place it occurred and the names of witnesses.

Your safety

The UK is generally a safe place to study and live, but, as in any country, it is important to take precautions to ensure your security. Below are some tips to help you protect yourself and your belongings against crime.

Safety in the home

- Keep your home secure at all times. Lock it when you go out. Install good quality locks on doors and windows. If you live in a Halls of Residence, lock your window and door when you leave, even if you only go down the corridor. Be careful about who you let into the Halls of Residence.
- Never leave keys in obvious places such as inside the letterbox, or under plants and doormats. Hide valuable items so that they cannot be seen through the windows.

(Continued)

- Use only electrical and gas appliances that are safe and in working-order. Turn them off when not in use. Ask your landlord to confirm that gas and other appliances are safe; ask to see a record of safety checks and safety certificates.
- Install a burglar alarm and smoke alarm in your home.
- If you leave your home for a few days, ask a friend to open and close curtains, and collect the post. Buy a timer-switch for lights to give the impression you are not away.
- Your university may be able to provide safety storage for your belongings when you return to your country during vacations or go on holiday.
- Property can be marked using a permanent or ultra violet marker with your name and address.

Safety outside
- Be vigilant and aware of your surroundings when you go outside.
- Be aware of pick-pockets and bag-snatching. Do not keep money in a back pocket, and do not leave belongings unattended. Try to avoid carrying large amounts of cash.
- Avoid obvious use of a mobile phone and other items such as personal stereos. Make a note of your phone's IMEI number (if your phone is stolen, you can report the number to the phone network to stop the phone being used).
- Try not to walk alone at night. Use well-lit and busy roads, and avoid short-cuts, such as in dark alleys and parks. Face on-coming traffic when walking on the pavement, and pay attention to cars that park alongside you.
- Be aware of people around you when you use a cash machine. Memorise your PIN number (never write it down), and do not keep cheques and cards together. Make a note of your account details, and keep them in your home in case they are stolen.
- Carry a personal alarm – some universities give them away for free!
- Avoid groups of people you don't know. When you go out, tell someone where you are going and the time you will come back.
- Be careful when crossing roads, and try to use a pedestrian crossing.
- Wait at well-lit stops or train platforms. It is safer to sit in busy compartments, downstairs on double-decker buses, and close to the driver.
- Do not leave drinks unattended, and do not accept drinks from strangers.

Safety on campus
- Attend safety training provided by your university and department.
- Comply with the university's health and safety regulations, and read relevant notices on campus.
- Report accidents that occur on campus to your university's health and safety team. They monitor incidents and prevent them from reoccurring.

- Inform security staff if you are in university in the evening or weekends.
- Familiarise yourself with the location of fire alarms, exits, access points, fire-fighting equipment, and the fire procedure. Evacuate buildings if you hear a fire alarm.

Car and bicycles

- Lock your car when you leave it, and put items out of sight. Lock all doors when you are alone in the car.
- Park your car in a well-lit open place or in an attended car park.
- Never keep keys in the ignition.
- Consider using security devices such as a wheel lock or engine immobiliser.
- Keep a torch in your car in case it breaks down in the evening or night.
- Mark equipment, such as the car stereo, with your name, address, and vehicle registration number.
- Plan your route before you set off.
- Always lock your bicycle to an immovable object such as a bike rack. You may be able to take away removable parts.
- Mark the bicycle's frame, and make a note of the model, manufacturer, and frame number.
- Wear a bicycle helmet and suitable clothing.

If you are attacked

- Try to stay calm. Evaluate the situation.
- If someone tries to steal your bag, it may be better to let them to do so rather than fight. If you are attacked, try to run away, and attract attention by screaming or using a personal alarm.
- Remember as much information as possible about the situation, such as the details of the attacker.
- Call the police immediately, and report the incident to your university. You may also want to contact the university's counselling service for support.

In an emergency

Dial 999 in an emergency (for example, when someone's life is threatened or a crime is in progress). Non-emergency crime should be reported to your local police station as soon as possible; there may be a police officer assigned to your university. The police can also provide helpful advice about crime prevention.

7 Academic culture in the UK

INTRODUCTION

After reading this chapter, you should:

☑ Understand how universities and courses are organised
☑ Know your responsibilities as a student
☑ Know about research degrees and what they involve
☑ Succeed as a part-time or mature student

This chapter explains how universities and their courses are organised. There is information about how the academic year is structured, the staff who will teach and support you, and your responsibilities as a student. Research degrees, and their differences to taught courses, are also explained, and there are tips for mature and part-time students.

Organisational structure of universities

The leader of a university is called a Vice-Chancellor (also known as a President, Principal, or Chairperson). He/she is supported by a Deputy Vice-Chancellor or Pro-Vice Chancellor. They have overall responsibility for the leadership and management of their university. The day-to-day running of a university is done through two general teams of staff:

- *Academic teams* which consist of faculties that are further divided into departments or schools.
- *Management and administrative teams* that are organised into departments (or Directorates), e.g., Finance, Human Resources, Registry, International Support Office.

A university is governed and advised by various committees. The chief governing bodies are the Court, Council, Senate, and various others.

- *University Court*. The highest governing body. It consists of a large number of university staff and community representatives who meet once a year to discuss the university's affairs.
- *University Council*. Responsible for setting strategy, overseeing finances, planning, resource allocation, and other business. Ensures that the university fulfils its legal and external responsibilities.
- *Senate*. Directs policies about admissions, teaching, research, examinations, and enterprise. Responsible for assuring academic quality and standards. Its members consist of deans, departmental heads, professors, and other academic staff.

There are opportunities for students to participate as student representatives (see below), in university committees such as the Council, Senate, and smaller committees such as departmental meetings.

Becoming a student representative

Student representatives represent the views of their fellow students at university meetings. They act as a communication channel between students and staff. A student who has feedback or a problem to discuss can ask their representative to raise the issue at a relevant meeting. For example, your university may have an International Student Representative who helps other international students to voice their opinion or concern about life as a student. Student representatives also inform and consult students about any plans or changes within the university.

Opportunities to be a representative are usually announced by departments, such as on notice boards. Alternatively, you can contact your course director or departmental secretary. There are several benefits of being a student representative. They enable you to:

- make an important contribution to your department or university
- develop new skills, such as communication skills, participating in meetings, etc.
- get involved in the running of the university
- gain experience that will look good on your CV.

Student representatives are usually elected by other students and serve for a year. The amount of time they spend on duties varies, although many committees meet only a few times each year.

Academic year and week

The time period between when you begin and finish your studies each year is known as the 'academic year'. It generally begins in September or October and ends in June or July. The academic year consists of two semesters or three terms that are separated by vacations, and is between 30 and 40 weeks in duration.

The first term or semester begins with registration and enrolment on courses, and induction. The first semester is proceeded by a winter (Christmas) vacation, then semester two (Spring semester) and then a summer vacation. Exams are held at the end of each semester.

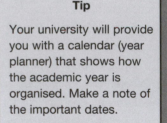

Tip

Your university will provide you with a calendar (year planner) that shows how the academic year is organised. Make a note of the important dates.

There is a lengthy vacation in the summer in which you can return to your country, travel around the UK and Europe, or work. However, some postgraduate taught courses and research degrees do not have a summer vacation and the time is used for academic activities, such as undertaking a dissertation. In addition to the winter and summer vacations, there are also holidays at Easter and in May. Some universities offer flexible arrangements, such as courses that begin in the second semester, or the use of the summer vacation as an additional semester in order to shorten courses.

On a full-time course, you should expect to spend between 35–40 hours a week on your studies, which includes about 15–25 hours of formal class time. The remainder is independent study, e.g., reading lecture notes and books, and completing coursework. The workload will differ from week-to-week, depending on class arrangements, the amount of class preparation you need to do, and when your tutors set assignments.

Course structure

Most courses are modular. This means that they are divided into self-contained units of study known as modules or units. A module is studied during a single semester. Each module has a 'credit rating', such as 10, 20, and 30 credits, which indicates the amount of learning that is involved and its level of difficulty. It is generally agreed that one credit is equal to 10 hours of learning activity, including classes, independent study, and assessment. Therefore, courses with higher credit ratings require more classes as well as other learning activities, such as reading books and writing assignments. A module needs to be passed in order for credits to be awarded for it, and you will accumulate credits as you progress through a programme of study.

To complete a three-year undergraduate honours degree, you are expected to complete modules totalling 360 credits (120 credits each year; 60 per semester). Students who do not complete their degree course may be eligible to receive a lower award, such as a Diploma in Higher Education or Foundation degree (requires 240 credits), or a Certificate in Higher Education (requires 120 credits).

A postgraduate Master degree requires 180 credits, whereas a Postgraduate Diploma requires 120, and a Postgraduate Certificate requires 60. Doctorates are generally not credited, although some professional doctorates use the modular and credit system. An Integrated Master degree programme, which is a four-year undergraduate programme, requires 480 credits.

The modular course structure has several advantages. It enables courses to be flexible, so that students can choose different modules that match their interests and area they wish to specialise in. Modules can be compulsory or optional and can be chosen from a range of subjects, including modules from outside your immediate area of study. Credits are on nationally agreed scales, which mean they can be transferred between universities. The modular system also means that the total time required to study for a degree or other qualification is roughly the same for all students, regardless of the subjects they study.

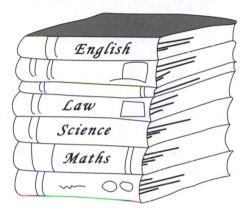

Credit Transfer

If you have already been awarded credits as part of a study programme, you may be able to transfer them to another university. This means the credit will count towards the qualification you want to study in the UK. It may also reduce the number of courses you will need to take. Some universities in the UK may be willing to recognise previous work experience as credit, especially if it is relevant to the course.

To apply for credit transfer, you must provide evidence that you have successfully completed a course (usually by providing an academic transcript that shows your results and credit rating), and provide information about its academic content. The credits that can be transferred may need to be related to the course you want to study. Bear in mind that transferred credits may prevent you from studying a module that is similar in content to it. Advice is available from admissions tutors and the department at the university you would like to study at.

Faculties, departments and their staff

A university's teaching and research staff are organised into several faculties, which are further divided into departments (also known as divisions or schools). Each faculty is led by a Dean or Principal, and each department has a Head or Coordinator. Courses are taught and managed by a range of academic staff:

- *Professor.* A senior teacher and researcher who is recognised for their scholarly achievements.
- *Reader.* A reputable researcher who is recognised for their scholarship.
- *Senior (Principal) Lecturer.* An experienced teacher who has several years' teaching experience.
- *Lecturer or Tutor.* A new or recently qualified teacher. Teaches students and conducts research.
- *Postdoctoral staff.* Someone who recently completed their doctoral degree and is continuing with their research.
- *Teaching Fellow/assistant.* A junior staff member who participates in teaching and perhaps research.
- *Visiting staff.* Does not have a permanent job in the university and stays in the department for a short time.
- *Honorary staff.* Occasionally teaches and conducts research in the department, but is not employed by the univerity.
- *Research Assistant.* Works on research projects with lecturers and professors.
- *Research student.* Postgraduate students who study for a research degree.
- *Administrative and technical staff.* Provides secretarial and specialist services for staff and students.

If you have a question or problem relating to a specific course, then you should see or email the staff member who teaches or coordinates it. Tutors are very busy, so it is best to ask questions during class or to make an appointment. Some tutors have fixed office hours each week in which they are available to meet students. Each faculty or department will have an office (called the Faculty Office) that can answer queries about aspects such as registration, timetables, lecture rooms, exam results, etc.

Many universities have a personal tutor system in which each student is assigned to a staff member who serves as a regular point of contact. The role of a personal tutor is to meet you regularly, discuss your progress, and to provide support and guidance about academic and non-academic problems that you encounter. You can see your personal tutor if you need help or want to talk about issues that are affecting your studies.

Support staff and services

There is a variety of other university staff whom you can meet for advice and support.

- *Accommodation officer.* Deals with applications for university-owned accommodation.
- *Admissions tutor.* Considers applications from students, and answers questions about admission to the university.
- *Careers advisor.* Helps students to think about and plan their career options.
- *Counsellor.* Provides confidential help and advice about any personal or academic concerns.
- *Chaplain.* Offers a pastoral service to students of all faiths. Arranges religious services.

- *Computing staff*. Provide support with computing and IT facilities, including Internet, email, and printing. They may offer training courses to help students learn how to use computer programs.
- *Disability officer*. Gives advice and support for students with learning disabilities and other disabilities.
- *English language and study skills tutors*. Teach academic English and study techniques.
- *Finance officer*. Receives payment of tuition and other fees, and provides advice about scholarships.
- *International student advisor*. Offers advice and support about a range of issues for international students, such as immigration, extending visas, etc.
- *Registry staff*. Help students to register with the university and department.
- *Mentor*. A member of staff or senior student who provides advice and support to help students settle in to university life.

There are also specialist services for mature students, students with disabilities, and for students with families.

Your responsibilities as a student

It is your responsibility to conduct yourself in a considerate and appropriate manner to follow the law, and to respect other people's rights. This includes abiding by the university's rules and procedures. Below is an overview of your responsibilities as a student. Refer to your student handbook and university's website for their policies.

- *Rules and regulations*. When you register at your university, you must agree to abide by the university's rules and regulations.
- *Attendance*. You are expected to attend all or most of your classes. Inform the university if you are unable to attend.
- *Study*. Take responsibility for your studies. This involves spending the required time each week to complete your work, and managing your learning. You are required to find out about assessment methods and the dates of exams.
- *Administration*. There are several administrative requirements to follow, such as course enrolment and registration, changing and withdrawing courses, etc. Check notice boards and email regularly, and inform the university if you change your address.
- *Health and safety*. Every student is expected to take reasonable care for the health and safety of themselves and other people, and to follow the university's health and safety regulations.
- *Finances*. Students are expected to pay their fees and other financial obligations.
- *Immigration*. Abide to immigration conditions associated with your student visa.
- *Equal opportunities*. Every student has a responsibility to treat others with respect and to support equal opportunity in the university campus (see below).

You will be given a 'student handbook', which provides important details about the university facilities you can use and the regulations you should abide to. It gives details about academic and support services, administrative procedures, and your responsibilities as a student. It is vital that you read the handbook and keep it for further reference. You will also receive a course booklet for each course that describes the course content and the location of lectures.

University policies and regulations

Every university has policies and regulations that govern the way it is run and that set the standards of appropriate behaviour of students and staff. They help to provide a safe and productive academic environment; policies also ensure that students and staff comply with the law.

The way that universities are run and the rules concerning your responsibilities may be very different to your country. It therefore is very important that you familiarise yourself with the university's rules and regulations so that you understand what is expected of you.

Equal opportunites

Universities in the UK are committed to providing equal opportunities for their students. They have a written policy to ensure that they actively promote equal opportunities and monitor how they achieve it. This means that all students should be treated equally, irrespective of attributes such as age, disability, ethnic group, gender, race, nationality, sexual orientation, etc. No student should receive less favourable treatment in services such as teaching, learning and assessment, and other support. Universities actively promote equal opportunities, and challenge unfair treatment. Your university will have a procedure for you to follow if you have any complaint about unfairness. Chapter 6 provides some suggestions about how to deal with unfairness.

Research degrees

The UK has a distinguished research reputation. In addition to teaching, many university lecturers conduct research and communicate their findings by writing articles, books, and giving talks. Some professors are world experts in their area. Many international students study research degrees to develop their skills and take advantage of the country's research facilities and expertise.

Most undergraduate and postgraduate courses will have a research component, in the form of a research project and dissertation in the final semester. Some postgraduate courses are entirely research based, such as MPhil and PhD degrees.

What is a research degree?

A research degree or diploma involves an in-depth investigation of a topic under the supervision of one or two experienced researchers (who are, usually, university lecturers). It includes considerable training to develop research skills. There are several differences between research and taught degrees:

- *Fewer lectures*. Most research degrees have few taught courses (e.g., a training programme about research methods and techniques). However, professional doctorates and Integrated PhDs have a significant taught element.
- *Independence*. You will work alone on a specialised topic, although you could be part of a research team. In many cases you can choose your field of study, and you will be responsible for developing your research enquiry and devising research methods to use. Research degrees are less structured than taught courses, which means that you can decide how and when to do the research.
- *A thesis*. The results and conclusions of a research project are written up in a long report, called a thesis. The length of the thesis varies between disciplines.
- *Oral examinations*. A thesis is assessed by an external examiner. The assessment method for research degrees involves an oral exam, known as a *viva voce*.
- *Teaching*. There may be opportunities to undertake part-time teaching and other duties alongside your research. This will help you to develop skills in these areas, improve your CV, and earn extra money.

Why study for a PhD (or DPhil)?

A PhD is a doctoral research degree that involves a detailed investigation and evaluation of a topic and leads to the creation of new knowledge. It requires advanced research techniques and academic enquiry. Students who successfully complete a PhD become an authority on the subject, and are competent to work on other research topics. There are several reasons why you may be interested in studying for a research degree:

- you enjoy a subject and want to deepen and broaden your knowledge of it
- develop research skills
- improve your career and job prospects
- research is intellectually stimulating
- the UK has excellent research facilities and supervision.

Entry requirements

To study for a research degree, you will need to have an undergraduate degree (a first or upper second honours) or a Master's degree, English language qualifications, and research experience. Applicants who do not have a Master degree register initially for an MPhil and then apply to be considered for a transfer to a PhD. Entrance requirements vary widely between universities.

Table 7.1   Types of research courses

There are different postgraduate research degrees. They differ in their aims, duration, level of analysis, and amount of research involved.

Type of course	Characteristics	Length of thesis	Duration (full-time)
Doctor of Philosophy (PhD or DPhil)	A detailed investigation and evaluation of a topic that leads to an original and significant contribution to knowledge. Findings should be publishable in academic journals and/or a book.	70,000–100,000 words	3–4 years
Master of Philosophy (MPhil)	Similar to a PhD, but more limited in scope. Usually studied as a foundation to a PhD.	50,00–70,000 words	1–2 years
Research diploma (e.g.PGDip)	Involves the investigation of a topic, development of research methods, and submission of a thesis (but in less depth than an MPhil).	20,000 words	9–18 months
Integrated PhD	An interdisciplinary degree that includes taught courses, a research project, and the development of professional and research skills.	Variable	3–4 years
Professional doctorate	Includes taught courses, and emphasises the application of knowledge to issues that are relevant to the student's career.	Variable. Around 50,000 words	Variable
Masters by research (e.g. MA/MSc/ MRes)	Similar to a taught Masters degree (see Chapter 1), but includes a significant amount of research.	15,000–40,000 words	1 year
PhD by portfolio	Involves the completion of a portfolio that consists of work-related projects, along with a written report.	Variable	Variable

How can I choose a topic and supervisor?

Think carefully about choosing your topic, supervisor, and university. They will influence your enjoyment and success on your course. Also think about how your studies will be funded, and how and where you can apply for scholarships.

There are many research areas that you can specialise in. Students can choose their own research area and supervisor, although the choice will be restricted if applying for a funded position in which supervision arrangements have been pre-arranged.

You can begin by identifying topics that interest you, and then look into them further. Find out details about university staff who have research interests similar to yours.

Research degrees are supervised by one or two experienced staff who are experts in the area. The role of a supervisor is to provide guidance about how to do research, to ensure that appropriate research methods are used, and to provide support and guidance. One supervisor will serve as a Director of Studies, and will provide overall direction for the research, whereas the second supervisor provides extra support about academic and pastoral issues.

Consider carefully the supervisor(s) you choose. It is important to get a good match between your needs and expectations and the type of support they can provide.

> **Tip**
>
> Universities vary in the types of research topics they can supervise. Learn about the research interests of departments and their staff by reading prospectuses and browsing their websites. It is important to fully explore your options before making a choice

Think about what you want from a supervisor. There are several factors to consider:

- *Research activity and reputation*. Some supervisors are leading experts in their areas. They may have published their work widely, be on the editorial boards of academic journals, and lead a research team.
- *Accessibility and support*. Check that supervisors will be accessible when you need advice. Do they have enough time to take you on? Some professors, especially eminent ones, have many students and cannot spend much time with each one.
- *Expertise*. Confirm that the supervisor has knowledge of the topics and research methods you intend to investigate and use.
- *Attitudes, personality and manners*. Every supervisor has their own way to respond to issues and to coach their students. One way to find out more is to talk to their existing or previous students.
- *Career outcomes*. Consider the career outcomes and success of previous students who have studied with the same supervisor and on similar topics.
- *Research culture*. Find out about the research activity of the department and university. Factors to consider include the presence of research teams and centres, number of research students, quality of journal papers and other publications, and amount of research funding. It is also useful to check a department's RAE rating (see Chapter 1).

Communicating with your supervisor

It is important to have regular contact with your supervisor. The amount of contact you have will depend on your preferences, ability, discipline, and stage of the research project.

If the rapport between you and your supervisor breaks down, then you can first discuss the problems together. If the situation does not improve, you could seek advice from another member of the department. Your university will have a formal procedure to resolve any problem. One option, as a last resort, is to change a supervisor.

Common problems with supervisors include:

- lack of support
- not enough time for you
- disagreement about the direction of the research
- personality clash.

It is worth bearing in mind that you might be allowed to conduct part of the research in your own country, especially if your topic concerns it. You will be expected to arrange local support and facilities, and to maintain regular contact with your supervisors. Some universities offer joint arrangements and programmes with universities in other countries. This means you can spend most of your time at the university in your country, and have a supervisor there.

Assessment

Supervisors monitor the progress of their students. This will take place in formal meetings at regular intervals to evaluate your work. You might be given a personal development plan that details the tasks you need to do, and a learning contract that sets out the university's expectations regarding your performance on the research programme. These measures are to help you progress and complete the research degree.

The formal assessment of a research degree includes an oral examination (known as a viva or thesis defence), in which examiners will ask questions about the thesis. At a viva, you will be required to explain and defend your research against their questions. There are two examiners; an external examiner, who is an expert in the field and from another university, and an internal examiner from your university.

The aim of the viva is to ensure that:

- the work is your own
- you understand the field
- you can justify the research methods you used
- your reasoning and assumptions are sound
- the data analysis and presentation is appropriate
- there is an original and significant contribution to knowledge
- you know the limitations and future directions of your research.

Supervisors are able to attend the viva, but will not be able to participate unless invited to do so by the examiners.

There are several ways to prepare for a viva. Since the thesis is submitted several months before, it is important to read it again to thoroughly understand its contents.

- read each chapter of the thesis and summarise the main points.
- understand the topic, both in a wider context as well as the specific focus covered in the thesis
- ensure that you understand the rationale of the research – be able to explain why you used certain research and data analysis methods
- understand the original contribution to knowledge
- be familiar with the references cited in the thesis
- identify controversial and debatable statements in the thesis
- anticipate questions the examiners could ask
- ask your supervisor for a mock exam.

After the viva, there are several outcomes the examiners could choose:

- award the degree, either with no changes required in the thesis or minor corrections
- ask you to make major corrections and resubmit the thesis to be re-examined
- award a lower degree
- award no degree.

Being a mature or part-time student

Universities welcome students of all ages. Although most students go to university directly after they finish secondary school, a large proportion decide to return to study after gaining work experience, raising a family, or even after retirement! The number of mature students is increasing every year.

Reasons for returning to study

Returning to study, especially in another country, is a big decision. There are many reasons why you could be thinking about being a mature student. They include, to:

- improve your career and job prospects
- make up for opportunities that you missed when you were younger
- make a fresh start in your life
- develop transferable skills
- study a subject that interests you
- gain personal satisfaction.

Entrance requirements

Standard entry requirements for courses apply to school leavers. Requirements are more flexible for mature students because their work and life experiences are taken into consideration. The skills that you have developed during your job, childcare, and voluntary activities indicate your ability to succeed at university. Admissions tutors will look at your previous work and life experience for evidence of your skills, commitment, motivation, and ability to work independently.

> **Tip**
>
> If you do not have formal qualifications, contact your university for advice. Every application from a mature student is considered on its own merits.

If you find that your background does not qualify for entry on to a degree course, then don't worry; there are other options. For example, you could consider studying an access course or foundation programme in the UK, which is a course specially designed to prepare adult learners for higher education. There are also other courses that can qualify you for university study.

Adjusting to university life

Returning to education is a big step. It will change your lifestyle and the people around you. Mature students may need to leave their family for the duration of the course, or take their family with them.

Prepare yourself for returning to study by understanding what your courses will involve and what is expected of you. Consider the possible problems you could face. Think about how you will balance your studies with other commitments.

Confidence

There is a tendency for mature students, particularly those without formal qualifications or who have not studied for a long time, to feel anxious and to doubt their ability. Try not to think in this way! Remember that the skills and qualities that you have gained through your work and life experience have prepared you for the course, and will give you advantages. During your working life you have developed a range of skills that are essential for academic success.

If you do encounter any difficulties, remember that there are support services at university to help you. Try not to underestimate yourself – for example, most new students lack study skills and time-management skills, and acquire them as their course progresses.

Part-time study

Many full-time courses can be studied part-time, but there are visa and immigration requirements that prevent most international students from doing so. There are several advantages if you are able to study part-time, such as the opportunity to do other things such as to take care of a family. There are drawbacks of part-time study. They include:

- little time for hobbies and socialising with friends
- difficulties accessing university facilities, particularly in the evenings and weekends
- inability to attend classes because they clash with other commitments
- sustaining motivation over a longer period.

Think carefully about part-time study before you make a decision. It is worth speaking to other part-time students to learn about their experiences.

Ten tips for mature and part-time students

Below are some suggestions to help mature and part-time students plan their studies.

1 Learn about what university is like. A good starting point is to read this book!
2 Make sure that you are mentally prepared to be a university student. Think about why you want to study, the benefits and problems you could encounter, and how

(Continued)

well you will cope. If you are not ready for a course, consider a preparation course (e.g., an Access or Foundation course).

3 Remember that it takes time to adjust to the university environment and routine. It is particularly challenging during the first few weeks. Be patient, and keep persevering!

4 Make friends with other mature students on your course or in the same department. The university may organise a mentor scheme to put you in touch with a mature student who can give advice and encouragement.

5 Assess your abilities. Although you may not have formal qualifications, you have developed skills such as taking responsibility for your learning, self-motivation, time-management, and an ability to work things out for yourself. Think about the skills you have and how they relate to the course.

6 Find out whether university services are available at off-peak times.

7 Make all arrangements (such as childcare) before your course begins. Don't leave them to the last minute!

8 Learn how to use a computer. Almost all courses nowadays involve the use of computers. It will be less stressful if you know how to use computer packages, surf the Internet, and read email before the course begins.

9 If you are struggling with any aspect of your academic or personal life, then make use of your university's services, such as the counselling and health service, learning support, etc. See Chapter 6 for more information about your health and welfare.

10 There may be a society for mature students or a representative who can offer help and support. Join it and go along to their meetings.

8 Teaching and assessment methods

INTRODUCTION

After reading this chapter, you should:

- ☑ Be familiar with university teaching methods
- ☑ Understand how your work will be assessed
- ☑ Get the most out of your lessons
- ☑ Know what to do if you fail an exam

Courses vary in how they are taught and assessed. This chapter introduces the teaching and assessment methods used by universities, and helps you to get the most out of your lessons, exams, and coursework. There is also information about degree classifications and graduation.

How you will be taught

Common teaching methods used at university are lectures, tutorials, seminars, practical work, field work, laboratory sessions, work placements, and online learning. The way you will be taught at university level is different to secondary school. At university you are expected to take responsibility for your learning; you are in charge of the number of lessons you attend, how to supplement course materials with additional reading, and managing your time and activities. This level of independence is very different to secondary school, where your teachers told you what and how to study.

Lectures

Lectures are the main teaching method for undergraduate courses. A lecture is like a large class in which a teacher (known as a lecturer) gives an oral presentation about a topic. The aim of a lecture is to:

- explain the main points of a course
- provide information about a topic

- discuss recent developments and up-to-date research findings
- stimulate your interest
- provide a framework for your thinking and discussion.

Lectures typically last about 50 minutes, although they can last as long as 3 hours. They are attended by large groups of students – from 20 to several hundred.

Lectures are one-way communication, with the lecturer explaining information to students. Good lecturers will involve their audience in their lessons by, for example, asking questions and asking them to complete activities.

Audio-visual aids are used to enhance understanding of the content presented. They include PowerPoint, flip charts, white board, overhead projector, and video. It is usual for students to be given a handout that summarises the lecture.

Getting the most out of your lectures

There are several things you can do to increase your learning in lectures.

- **Prepare for the lecture.** Read background information about the topic. You may be able to download slides in advance of the lecture from the course's virtual learning environment. It is also a good idea to preview your notes from previous lectures, including the new vocabulary covered. If you don't understand any of the material, prepare some questions to ask.
- **Practise your listening skills.** Practise your listening skills, such as your ability to listen for general and specific details (e.g., main ideas, details, and keywords); understanding gist; and understanding speakers' opinions. Before each lesson, look at the glossary section in your textbook to practise new keywords.
- **Take notes.** Take brief notes about the materials covered in the lecture so that you can read and understand them in the future. Notes should be organised in a clear and logical form. See the next chapter for tips about how to improve your note-taking skills.
- **Be active!** Rather than passively listening to the lecturer, engage in the learning process. For example, pay attention to and think about the points the lecturer makes, and raise questions when appropriate. Find ways to link a lecture to your past lectures and experiences. After a lecture, find out more about the topic, rewrite your notes, and discuss the topic with your classmates.
- **Review and reflect.** After the lecture, read the notes and handouts to see what you did not understand. Read the relevant section of the textbook. Think about your learning during lectures and how it can be improved.

- **Recognise different teaching styles.** Each lecturer uses different teaching methods, audio-visual aids, and has a particular accent and pace. Try to recognise and become accustomed to each lecturer's style.
- **Attend as many lectures as possible.** Your attendance at lectures and other classes may or may not be monitored by your tutor. Even so, you should try to attend all of them. Some courses may have an attendance policy in which you must attend a certain number of classes to be able to pass the course.

Seminars and tutorials

In seminars and tutorials, small groups of students (less than 15) discuss and expand on the content covered in their lectures or additional reading material.

- *Tutorials* last for about an hour and provide an opportunity to discuss your general progress, give feedback on your work, and to talk about any problems you may have.
- *Seminars* are larger and more formal. They have a main speaker, who presents a topic to other students. You may be asked to give a seminar presentation during your course.

The main aims of seminars and tutorials are to:

- enhance understanding and share views about a topic
- develop your skills in oral presentation and team work
- give and receive constructive criticism
- develop confidence
- engage in discussion that will continue outside the seminar
- meet other students and make friends.

Seminars are a good way to give your ideas, and to discuss any areas that you do not understand. They are chaired by a lecturer, graduate students, or teaching assistants.

Seminars for postgraduates focus on discussion of research projects and findings. An official type of seminar is a conference, in which postgraduates and academic staff meet and present their research findings. Conferences are a good chance to network with other postgraduates and researchers.

Seminars are sometimes assessed. Assessment criteria could include how well you prepare, your contribution and interaction with other students, and your presentation skills. You could be asked to write a seminar paper, which is a record of the content covered in the seminar.

Participating in seminars

It is important to contribute to seminars, and to interact with the group.

Before
- Make sure that you know when and where the seminar will be held. Get to know the other group members beforehand.
- Prepare. Read the materials, and analyse the information for the seminar. Think about how it can be built into a discussion.
- Make a list of the points you would like to discuss, and take them to the seminar. Good preparation will also give you more confidence to ask and answer questions.
- Think about the purpose of the seminar, and what you want to gain from it.

During
- Arrive on time, and remember to take the notes you made when preparing.
- Do your best to contribute to seminars. Give your views, agree with or challenge other people's views, and ask questions.
- Actively listen to other students and pay attention.
- Make notes.
- Encourage others to join.

After
- Review your notes.
- Reflect on the experience. Think about your performance in the seminar and how you can improve it.

Practical, laboratory, and field work

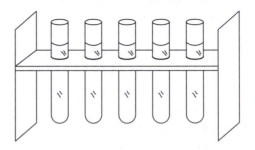

Practical work in laboratories, studios, and workshops is an essential part of science, media, and vocational courses. They allow 'hands on' experience and the development of practical skills. They enable students to:

- put the theories and concepts they learn in lectures into practise
- develop practical and observation skills and learn how to use equipment

- collect and analyse data
- learn about the scientific method; this includes formulating a hypothesis and conducting experiments to validate or modify it.

Courses may include field work, such as trips to a local area or further away. They can last for a day or longer. You may be asked to contribute towards the cost of field work (in addition to tuition fees). Bear in mind that it is usually compulsory to attend practical lessons, and it is important to abide by health and safety regulations during them.

Distance and computer-based learning

Computers, particularly the Internet, are commonly used as a teaching method. Your university may use a Virtual Learning Environment (VLE), which is an online system that manages courses and enables communication between students and teachers. An example of a VLE used in UK universities is Blackboard, which provides students with course details such as lecture notes, timetables, and tests. It also has tools for communication between classmates and tutors, such as discussion boards and a live chat.

There will be computer facilities for you to use in your university and department. They include a computer network, Internet and email access, and facilities such as printing and scanning. Many degree programmes provide training in IT skills – if not, ask your library or university computing centre if they offer short courses.

Some universities offer distance learning courses to enable students to study without attending class. This means that there is no requirement to be present in the classroom. The quality, structure and content of distance learning courses are virtually the same as courses studied in class. Students can learn course material via a variety of channels, including:

- correspondence through regular mail
- books
- Internet (e.g., websites, blogs, and bulletin boards)
- radio and television
- CD-ROM
- email support from tutors.

Some courses are entirely taught via distance learning, whereas others have attendance requirements. They are convenient for students who live far from a university or have other commitments, such as a job or family. However, distance learning courses are not a popular option for international students who go to the UK to study; if you are interested, check the requirements of your visa.

Work placements

Some courses, particularly vocational ones, include work placements. A work placement is a period of time spent in a commercial or public organisation to complete tasks for an employer. The type and duration of work placements vary between universities and courses. They could be an optional or integral component of degree programmes. They can be short-term (a few days or several weeks) or long-term (e.g., one-year in duration). A sandwich course is an undergraduate degree that has a one-year work placement, taken in the third year of a four-year programme.

Work placements enable students to learn about aspects of a subject that they cannot attain in class:

- opportunities to understand academic concepts and apply them to real world situations
- increase your chances of finding a job after graduation (because employers value practical experience)
- develop employability and transferable skills
- find out about the type of jobs you like
- increase enthusiasm and motivation for your course
- make you aware of the problems you will face in employment, such as working pressure and other constraints.

Placements are in partnership, or closely tied, with your university. The university will plan and coordinate the work placement (a designated member of staff in your department or faculty will do this). The university will prepare you for the work placement, and a member of staff will visit you there several times. There is also an external supervisor based in the company.

Not all courses and universities find work placements for students and you may need to search and apply for one yourself. Some universities allow work placements to be done in other countries, but you should check the immigration rules for any restrictions. If your course does not allow a work placement, think about other work experience during your vacations.

A work placement can be an assessed part of a course. Assessment criteria include progress on and completion of the placement, and coursework such as an assignment, a project, keeping a diary, writing a dissertation, or compiling a portfolio.

Tuition fees may need to be paid during the placement, although they will likely be reduced. Make sure to check any immigration restrictions on undertaking work placements and experience.

Success in your work placement

Your success in a work placement depends on how well you prepare for it and settle-in. Below are some suggestions to help you get the most out of it.

- Before you choose a work placement, think about what you want to learn, and the types of careers and jobs you are looking for. Choose a placement that satisfies these interests.
- Attend a preparation class organised by your university. It will help you get ready for the work placement. Before you begin the placement, learn about the employer and the job.
- You may need to apply for the placement by sending a CV and an application form, or attending an interview. Your university's career's centre should also be able to help you write your CV and practise interview techniques.
- Be clear about the terms of the placement, including the duration, duties, length, job description, working hours and conditions. Also, understand and complete the academic requirements of the placement, such as assessed work.
- Be professional during the placement. You should be punctual, and follow the company's rules, such as the dress code. Keep a positive attitude in your work, and do your best to make a contribution to the company.
- After you complete the placement, ask the company for feedback about your performance and how you can improve. Think about your strengths and weaknesses and how you can develop them further.

How you will be assessed

Many courses have examinations at the end of each semester as well as continuous assessment that consists of assignments. Courses vary in the proportion of the final mark accounted for by exams and continuous assessment.

Details about assessment methods for each course are available from your teacher and your degree programme handbook. It is important that you understand how you will be assessed, including the number of assignments you need to complete, the deadlines, and the assessment rules and procedures.

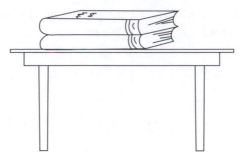

What is an assignment?

An assignment is a piece of coursework that you should complete during your course. It can be an:

- examination
- essay or report
- project
- oral presentation
- portfolio
- seminar presentation
- dissertation or thesis
- display or performance.

☑ **Checklist for handing in an assignment**

Below are some points to check when you write and hand in an assignment

Questions
- ❑ Answer the right questions
- ❑ Analyse the question title
- ❑ Read the assessment criteria
- ❑ Collect information from different sources
- ❑ Use evidence to support your views

Structure & Presentation
- ❑ Plan and organise your writing
- ❑ Use the correct structure
- ❑ Write a first draft and edit/proofread it

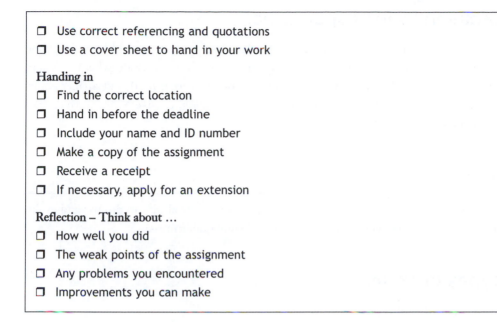

□ Use correct referencing and quotations

□ Use a cover sheet to hand in your work

Handing in

□ Find the correct location

□ Hand in before the deadline

□ Include your name and ID number

□ Make a copy of the assignment

□ Receive a receipt

□ If necessary, apply for an extension

Reflection – Think about …

□ How well you did

□ The weak points of the assignment

□ Any problems you encountered

□ Improvements you can make

Tutors use assignments to assess knowledge, skills and understanding. Work experience or professional practice included in the course is also assessed.

How can I get good marks?

Assignments vary in their type, length, and the time required to complete them. To get good marks for an assignment, there are several things you will need to think about:

- Analyse the meaning of the question (title) very carefully. It will show you what is required in the answer.
- Find out what your tutor is looking for. They should provide you with clear assessment criteria that will be used to mark your work.
- Give evidence and examples to support your views.
- Follow a specific structure and format.

Chapter 9 has tips to help you do well in assignments and to improve your study skills.

Handing in an assignment

Keep a note of the assignment deadlines. There will be a penalty for late submissions, such as a deduction in the number of marks you can achieve. See your tutor if you have a problem handing in work on time – you may be able to get an extension.

Lecturers' varied approaches

All tutors have their own preferences about how assignments should be written and presented. Follow the requirements set by each tutor. They include whether assignments must be word processed; the type and size of paper to be used; and smaller points such as whether you should use headings, double spacing, passive or active voice, and referencing methods, etc.

Exams

The aim of an exam is to test your knowledge; assess your ability to discuss and evaluate issues; and to test your ability to work and cope under pressure.

Types of exams

There are different types of exams:

- *Unseen exams*. A traditional type of exam in which students answer questions that they have not previously seen.
- *Seen/open questions*. Questions are given before the exam so that students can prepare the answers at home and write them in an exam.
- *Open book*. Books and other course materials can be taken into the exam room.
- *Oral (viva)*. Commonly used in language courses to test listening and speaking skills, or for the examination of a postgraduate research degree.
- *Practical*. Tests students' ability at hands-on tasks.

Exam timetable and exam room

An exam timetable is a schedule that lists the day, time, and location of exams. It is placed on the notice board and the intranet, and you may be issued with a personalised one. Remember to check you have been entered for the correct exams.

In the exam room, you must read, listen to, and understand the examination instructions and rules carefully. They will provide details about:

- the number of questions to answer
- the time you have
- whether answers should be written on the exam paper or in an answer book.

> **Tip**
>
> Special exam arrangements can be provided for students with a medical condition, a disability, visual impairment, or dyslexia. Ask the university for details.

Exam study skills

There are various techniques you can do to prepare for exams and improve your score. They include:

- planning your time
- selecting material to revise
- choosing appropriate study methods
- finding out about the exam
- practising with a mock exam
- planning your time and activities in the exam room.

Before you sit an exam, find out what you are allowed to take in to the exam room. The next chapter has an overview of exam skills and techniques.

Exam results

Summer exams are held in May and June, whereas the winter exam period is in December and January. Results are available about two months afterwards. You should receive a letter and transcript that lists your exam scores and the courses you have passed or failed. The exam scores are also available online.

Make sure that your university has your correct contact address, especially if you are returning to your country during the vacation. Inform your family that you are expecting a letter so that it does not get overlooked.

The pass mark varies between programmes, but is about 40 per cent for undergraduate courses, and 50 per cent for postgraduate courses.

Universities have a system to ensure that exam answers are marked fairly and accurately. Marked papers are checked by other staff and external examiners (teaching staff at other universities). External examiners check samples of assessed work and the suitability of exam questions. A sample of exam questions are also moderated, which means that a staff member checks that a sample of answers have been marked according to the standard marking scheme.

Academic misconduct (cheating)

It is important to understand and follow the university rules concerning assignments and examinations. If you are found guilty of cheating, the penalties are serious; they include the award of no marks, the need to repeat an exam or essay, or withdrawal from the university. In an exam, you must not:

- copy from or communicate with other students
- take unauthorised materials such as notes in the exam

- remove question papers and answer books unless authorised to do so
- take mobile phones or other communication devices into the exam room
- plagiarise (see p. 143)
- falsify experimental results
- ask another person to take the exam for you.

What can I do if I miss or fail an exam?

If you fail an exam, you should see your tutor or head of department as soon as possible to discuss the situation.

Resits

Students who fail an exam are usually allowed to re-sit it at a later date. However, in a re-sit exam the maximum score that can be achieved may be capped (e.g., at 40 per cent or 50 per cent). The number of times a student can re-sit an exam depends on the university's regulations. If a student fails a re-sit, then the department's Exam Committee may need to consider whether another re-sit is permitted. Alternative options include repeating the subject or terminating the course. There may be a registration process for re-sit examinations, and there will be a deadline and fee. If you have passed an exam but would like a higher score, you are unlikely to be allowed to sit the exam again, unless there are mitigating circumstances (see below).

Mitigating (extenuating) circumstances

Inform your university of any serious issue, such as illness, bereavement, or a personal issue that affected your exam performance or inability to take an exam. They are known as 'mitigating circumstances'. The departmental Exam Board may be able to take them into consideration. Mitigating circumstances do not include minor illness or a situation which could have been avoided by planning.

Compensation

In some courses, under certain circumstances, students may be given credits for a failed exam and proceed to the next year or to graduate. This is known as compensation. Further details can be found in your student handbook.

Preparing for a re-sit exam

- Think about why you failed the exam. Did you do enough revision? Was the exam too difficult? Think of ways to solve the problem.
- Start your revision early. It is also important to have a full set of exam notes (if they are incomplete, ask a classmate who achieved a high score for a copy of theirs!).
- Put a failed exam behind you; focus on any other exams you have.
- Some universities allow re-sit exams to be taken overseas at, for example, a British Council office.

Using feedback from lecturers

You will be given written and/or verbal feedback from your tutors about your assignments. Their comments are helpful because they provide guidance about how the assignment could be improved. Feedback will be written on the assignment or on a form (cover sheet). See your tutor if you would like further advice. Try not to be disappointed about negative and critical comments; view them as an opportunity to improve your skills.

Degree classifications and their importance

After you have successfully completed your degree programme, you will be awarded a qualification. Undergraduate degrees are graded to distinguish between students with different levels of achievement. Your grade, known as a classification, will be based on your overall performance on your degree programme (usually, only the second and third year are included in the calculation). Below is a commonly used classification scheme (Table 8.1).

The degree can be awarded with or without 'Honours'. The highest Honours that can be achieved is the First-Class Honours. The lowest level, the Pass degree without Honours, is awarded at the discretion of the Board of Examiners.

Master degrees are likely to be unclassified or classified as 'Pass, Merit, or Distinction'. Doctoral degrees are not classified, and the graduate is awarded only the title.

An 'Aegrotat degree' is a degree awarded to a candidate who was unable to take exams because of illness but who would have passed under normal circumstances.

Degree classification is important because it determines the options available to you after graduation. For example, a 2:2 is the entry requirement for a Master degree course, whereas Doctorates usually require a 2:1. Further, graduates with a 2:1 or First are in a stronger position to be accepted on to highly desirable postgraduate courses or to obtain a scholarship. Prospective employers also use degree classifications as an indicator of ability.

Table 8.1 Degree classifications

Grade (score)	Classification	Abbreviation
70–100	First-Class Honours	First or 1st
60–69	Upper Second-Class Honours	2:1
50–59	Lower Second-Class Honours	2:2
40–49	Third-Class Honours	Third or 3rd
Below 40	Pass (Ordinary degree without Honours)	Pass
0	Fail	--

Graduation – how to get your qualification

The final stage of your academic career is graduation, when you and your classmates are awarded with your degree or other qualification.

Graduation ceremony

You will have the chance to attend a graduation ceremony, known officially as a 'congregation for the conferment of degrees'. It is a special occasion when you can celebrate your achievement. Students who have successfully completed their studies can attend, and they are formally known as 'graduands'. Guests, such as family members, can also attend, but they may need to pay a fee, and most universities limit the number of guests per student to two or three. Summer graduation ceremonies are held in July, winter ceremonies are in January or February. If you wish to attend in the winter, make sure that your visa will not have expired before that time.

Graduation ceremonies take place in a large hall, such as in a cathedral. Graduands and academic staff wear academic dress at the ceremony, including a gown, hood, and cap, and smart clothes such as a suit. International students are also allowed to wear their national dress.

The graduation ceremony is divided into several stages:

1 Before the ceremony, you can go to a gowning room to put on your outfit.
2 You will be given a seat next to your classmates. Sit down until your name is called by a senior member of staff (the Chancellor or Vice-Chancellor).
3 You will then walk across the stage to shake hands with him/her.
4 You will be presented with a certificate or scroll at the ceremony, but it is not an official one and is used only for ceremonial purposes. Degree certificates will be sent to you, by recorded delivery, within a few months.

After the ceremony there will be a buffet or party where you can talk about the event and have fun!

Below are suggestions to help you prepare for your graduation day:

- Read the graduation booklet or pack from your university that explains the details of the ceremony.
- Buy or hire a graduation gown from a robe maker appointed by your university. You should be able to order them by phone and collect on the day of the ceremony. Before you order, know your chest and height measurements, and head circumference.

> **Tip**
>
> You must pay any debts you have to the university before you can graduate. They include unpaid tuition fees, fines, and unreturned library books.

- You should be given the option to have photographs taken, and to purchase a video (VHS or DVD) of the graduation ceremony.
- If your family will attend, remind them to apply for their visas and book flights and accommodation. It is advisable to make travel arrangements after your university has confirmed their attendance.

Further information is available from your university's Graduation Office.

Graduation in absentia

If you cannot attend the graduation ceremony, you can ask to defer your graduation and attend a later one. Alternatively, you can request for your qualification to be conferred in your absence. This is known as graduation *in absentia*.

See Chapter 10 for advice about life after graduation.

9 Study skills you need for academic success

INTRODUCTION

After reading this chapter, you should be able to:

- ☑ Understand a range of study skills and why they are used
- ☑ Identify your strengths and weaknesses
- ☑ Develop a plan to guide your learning
- ☑ Improve how you study

As you progress on your course, you will develop a range of study skills. These skills are essential for success at university, as well as in your future career. This section introduces a range of study skills and offers tips to help you improve your ability at them. There is also a checklist and a plan to help you to improve your learning.

What are study skills?

Success at university not only depends on gaining knowledge and memorising facts. It also depends on how well you can use and analyse the knowledge you learn. You will need to use information to write essays and reports, develop arguments, critically evaluate topics, give oral presentations, and work in groups. These attributes are known as 'study skills'. Study skills help students to improve their learning.

Other examples of study skills include time-management, taking notes from lectures, and preparing for exams. For example, time-management skills can help you to manage your work load; note-taking skills will help you to take adequate notes from your lectures; and exam and revision techniques will help you to improve your exam scores. Some countries place little emphasis on study skills, but they are an integral part of courses in the UK. It is important, therefore, for you to know about the types of study skills and to improve your ability at each one. A better understanding of these skills will help you to do well on your course.

Study skills are also essential in situations outside university, especially in your career. For this reason, they are known as 'transferable' skills (or 'soft' or 'employability' skills) as they can improve your performance in a job. When recruiting graduates, employers look for applicants that have skills such as the ability to communicate with others, work under pressure and in teams, organise their time, and meet deadlines. That these skills learnt in university can be transferred to the workplace is one of the reasons why many careers are open to graduates from various disciplines.

Different study skills

Courses differ with regard to the skills they require. For example, certain disciplines, such as science and engineering, place more emphasis on problem solving and report writing, whereas other courses such as teacher training and social work focus on professional competence. It is a good idea to find out which skills your course requires (look in your course handbook). The skills discussed in this chapter are used in many courses.

Tip

Recruiters will want to see evidence of the skills and abilities you developed while at university. Mention them on your CV, and be prepared to talk about them at job interviews.

Since this chapter serves as an introduction, you can browse other books and materials about study skills to explore them in greater detail. Another way to learn new skills is to attend a short course or workshop run by your university or local college.

Below is an introduction to a range of study skills and other attributes you will need for your course. This is followed by tips to help you develop each skill.

Table 9.1 Study skills

SKILL	DEFINITION
Active learning	Interacting with your course materials rather than passively reading them.
Critical thinking	Thinking about and reflecting on a view or argument being made, and analysing the evidence that supports it.
Essay and report writing	Substantial pieces of academic and formal writing that have a particular style, structure, and layout.
Independent learning	Taking responsibility for your studies, such as deciding how and when you learn; and planning and managing your learning.
Oral presentation	A talk to an audience. It requires good verbal and communication skills to demonstrate your knowledge and abilities.

(Continued)

Problem solving	Using a logical series of steps to help you think about ways to find a solution to a problem.
Referencing	Noting sources (known as references) that you use in your essays and reports to show where the facts and ideas came from.
Reflective learning	Assessing your strengths and weaknesses, including the way you learn, your effectiveness at studying, and factors blocking your performance.
Revision	Effective preparation for exams and coping with them.
Note-taking	Making effective notes from lectures, meetings, laboratory work, and from books and other resources you use.
Time management	Balancing academic work with other commitments. Using time more efficiently and effectively.

Essay and report writing

Students are often asked to write essays and reports. These are substantial pieces of formal writing (generally between 1500–2000 words) that explore issues in detail and demonstrate understanding of a topic. An extended type of report is a dissertation (thesis) which is done towards the end of a course – for bachelor and master degrees they can range from 5,000–25,000 words. Essay and report writing skills include: analysing the question; collecting information to write about; planning the structure; and then writing and editing.

How to structure an essay

The organization of your essay will depend on your course requirements. Most essays include four main sections: an introduction, a main body, a conclusion, and a reference list.

- *Introduction.* The introduction includes your interpretation of the essay title and provides brief background information to put the issue into context. You can also outline how you will answer the question, and introduce the issues that you will discuss.
- *Main body.* In the next section you should answer the question. Discuss the main issues relevant to the title. The paragraphs should have a logical order.
- *Conclusion.* The aim of the conclusion is to draw everything together and to summarise the main points. Refer back to the title to show the reader that the essay

question has been answered. You can express your own view based on the evidence discussed in the main body. It is also helpful to indicate areas that require further evaluation or research.

- *References*. It is important to write a list all of the books, articles and other materials that are mentioned in the essay (see page 142).

Analyse and understand the question

The meaning of the essay title (question) should be analysed very carefully so that you are clear about its purpose. The title will show you what is required in the answer, and will determine the way that you should write it. Essay titles include 'keywords' that indicate how the answer should be approached (for example, whether a topic should be 'described' or 'analysed'). Examples of keywords are: 'describe, discuss, evaluate, explain, compare and contrast, etc'. It is useful to underline the keywords in the title to remind you of what to focus on.

Collect information

The next step is to collect information to put in to your essay. There are many sources you can use, such as your lecture notes, books, journals, and newspapers. It is necessary to be selective – don't include too much or too little detail.

There will be a word or time limit, so you can't include all of the information you can find! You should critically think about the material you collect, such as whether it is useful, whether there is any bias, and if the source is reliable.

Plan and organise your writing

There are various ways to structure essays and reports. The common features are explained below.

How are essays and reports different?

Essays are used to describe or evaluate topics in detail, whereas reports present the results of an investigation or project. Reports are commonly used outside university, such as in business.

Essays and reports have a different structure. Reports have more sections and may include the analysis and presentation of data. Reports tend to be more concise and precise, and essays are more discursive and continuous.

Write, edit and proofread

You first need to write a draft, and then edit it to improve the content, style, and structure. Keep focused on the title and do not become sidetracked. Evidence and examples should be used to support your views - one way to do this is to discuss other people's research, and to include case studies, diagrams, graphs and tables.

Academic English should be used in essays; pay attention to your grammar and style. It is helpful to provide "signposting" (signs to help the reader through the essay or report), such as clear layout and headings. Think about appearance of the essay, such as whether your work should be word processed.

Structure of a report

Table 9.2 details a typical structure of a report. However, the structure varies across subjects and courses, and you should check the format that is required.

Oral presentation

You may be asked to give a talk to your class, or, if you are a research student, at a conference. Good presentations require good verbal and communication skills. It is important to use effective audio-visual aids; understand the audience; and to be able to deal with questions.

Table 9.2 Structure of a report

ELEMENT	DEFINITION
Title	A concise and accurate description of the report.
Abstract /summary	A summary and overview of all the main points of the report, including the aims, method, results, conclusions, and recommendations.
Acknowledgements	A brief note to thank people (e.g. colleagues, supervisors, or organisations) who helped during the report's compilation.
Contents	A list of the sections and their page numbers in the report.
Foreword	An explanation of the importance of the report.
Aims/objectives	A brief statement about the purpose and objectives of the report.
Introduction	Background details that put the issue into context. Includes a literature review about the topic. The aims and hypothesis of the study are usually stated.
Method	Description of how the study was conducted.
Results	Analysis of the data that were collected. May include graphs, tables, and maybe statistical analysis.
Conclusion	Data are interpreted and explained, and used to draw conclusions.
Recommendation	Solutions to any problems identified in the report. Indicates areas that require further research. The recommendations are used as a basis for making decisions.
References &/or bibliography	A list all of the books, articles and other materials used in the report. The reference section lists the sources. mentioned in the report, whereas a bibliography suggests additional material.
Appendix	Supplementary material or large amounts of data that are mentioned in the report but are not appropriate for inclusion in the main body.
Index	Lists the page numbers of each section and topic.

Good verbal and communication skills

Good communication skills are essential for giving a successful presentation.

- You should speak clearly and confidently.
- Your pace should not be too fast or too slow.
- It is better to talk from memory rather than read from notes. If you do decide to read, then it is better to use small cards.
- Non-verbal signals – such as body language and facial expressions – are important.

Understanding the audience

Every audience is different. They will differ in how much they know about the topic, their expectations, and their cultural background. These factors will influence the type of language you use in your presentation, the way you explain concepts, and your presentation materials. The presentation needs to be targeted towards the audience and their needs.

Try to build a rapport with the audience by greeting and talking to them (rather than looking at the screen), making eye contact, involving everyone, and asking questions to check that they understand.

Keep a look out for signs to show whether they are paying attention, have lost interest, or are confused. The audience can be kept interested by using humour, gestures, or demonstrations. Another way to attract their attention is to relate the content to their interests.

Effective audio-visual aids

Audio-visual aids include PowerPoint, flip charts, white board, overhead projector, and video. Effective audio-visual aids will help the audience to understand the presentation. They will also make your talk more interesting and professional. The aids need to be clear and brief. Check that the room has equipment to support the aids you want to use. You could consider writing a handout to give to the audience.

Structure and content

Like essays and reports, oral presentations should have a good structure, which includes an introduction, main body, and conclusion.

Presentations cover less detail than essays, so you will need to include only the main points. The aim and main argument need to be clear throughout the presentation, and the structure should show a logical progression. It is important to arrive on time and to keep to the time limit, which is usually between 10–20 minutes.

Characteristics of effective audio-visual aids

- visually pleasing
- clear and easily understood
- not too much detail
- font type, size and colour can be easily read
- only a few points on each slide
- graphs of an appropriate size and clearly labeled
- consistent layout in each slide

Verbal skills for presentations

- Speak slowly, clearly, and loudly
- Emphasise and repeat the main points
- Practice the pronunciation of difficult words before you give a presentation

Dealing with questions from the audience

It is common for the audience to ask questions. Answering them should not be a problem if you have prepared well. You can try to predict questions that could be asked (and prepare answers for them). If you don't know an answer to a question, be honest and say so. If no-one asks questions, you can encourage the audience by welcoming them, or by selecting someone. It is best to inform them at the beginning about whether they can ask questions during the presentation or if they should wait until the end.

Note-taking

During your studies you will need to take notes from lectures, books, and other materials.

Note-taking methods

There is no best way to take notes. You can develop your own style and format that suits you. Notes should be clear and logical so that they can be easily read and understood in the future. It is a good idea to number the pages of your notes, and to label them with the name and date of the lecture you take them from.

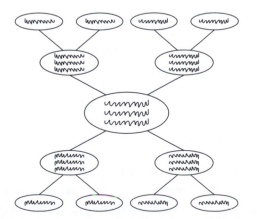

Two common note-taking styles are 'linear notes' and 'pattern notes'. Linear notes are written in sequential lines that start from the top of the page and then go down. In contrast, pattern notes are drawn using diagrams. One way to do this is to draw the main idea in a circle in the middle of the page, from which sub-ideas branch out in smaller circles (see opposite). Other diagrams – such as flow charts and tables – can be used. Coloured pens are useful to highlight key words and important points. You can, of course, use a mixture of note-taking styles.

It is a good idea to leave lots of space in your notes so that extra detail can be added later. This can be done by leaving gaps, using only one side of the paper, and writing on every second line.

Choosing appropriate content

Notes do not need to be written in full; don't write down every word your lecturer says. Save time by using your own words. Get into the habit of distinguishing between the lecturer's main points, examples, and repetition, and select only the information that is needed. If you are making notes from a book, read a whole chapter before you summarise it.

There are several ways to save time when note-taking:

- Eliminate verbs such as 'is, are, were' and pronouns such as 'they, that, them'. Notes can be understood without them, or you can add them after class.
- Use abbreviations to save time. For example, '&' instead of 'and', '=' for 'the same as/equal to'.
- List numbers as '1,2,3' instead of 'one, two, three'.

Organising your notes

Notes should be organised, up-to-date, and easily accessible. Loose-leaf notepaper is a good choice because it can be moved around and filed in folders. Other options include the use of small cards or a computer to store facts.

Review and edit your notes regularly. It is best to do it after class when the material is fresh in your mind. They can be supplemented with information from books, journals and other sources. Notes can be rewritten at a later date, or merged together with notes you take from other lectures and materials.

Time management

A challenging aspect of student life is balancing academic work with other commitments such as social activities, hobbies, a part-time job, and your family. Being able to juggle all of these tasks is a key factor in achieving academic success. Below are tips to help you manage your time.

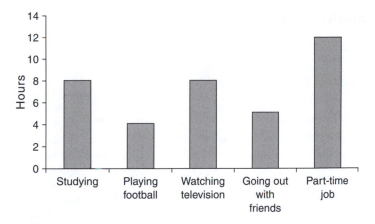

Documenting your time

Understand how you use time

The first step in achieving successful time management is to understand how you currently use your time. One way to do this is to construct a 'time log', which is a record of how you spend each hour of the day. At the end of each day and week you can use the log to find out where your time goes. You can add up the amount of time you spend on certain tasks, such as studying, watching television, eating, going out with friends, etc. This will help you to identify whether or not you are using your time for important tasks, or wasting large amounts on non-urgent activities.

The optimal study period before becoming restless is about 50 minutes, so plan breaks into your timetable.

Where do you study best? You may prefer to study in the library, at home, or even in the local park. There are other conditions that will also affect your study, such as people around you, and noise.

Make a plan and timetable

Being well-organised is an important part of good time management. Know the tasks that you need to do in the forthcoming week and plan ahead to do them:

- A timetable or diary will help you to plan your studies. Remember to include time slots for your hobbies and for relaxation.
- Allow time in your schedule for unforeseen events, and consider allocating more time for difficult tasks.
- Schedule time for preparation before class, and to review your notes after class.
- An action plan similar to that on page 149 – with a list of goals, activities, and timescales – will help you to track the things you need to do.

Time-saving tips

Below are other suggestions to help you manage your workload.

- *Divide big tasks into smaller ones*. This will help you to focus on each step at a time.
- *Prioritise to meet deadlines*. Although you have many things to do, some are more important than others. They can be put in to order of importance; the most urgent things can be done first. You may prefer to do the tasks you find most difficult at the time of day when you are at your peak for studying.

> **Tip**
> Understanding your study preferences will help you to arrange an effective environment to study in.

- *Assertiveness*. When you are busy, say 'no', to invitations for non-essential activities, such as social events.
- *Delegate*. Ask your friends or family to help with certain activities. For example, if your friend is going to the library, you could ask him/her to get the book that you want (to save you a trip to the library!).
- *Identify time-wasters*. Reduce and manage the things that waste your time, such as watching television or talking to friends on the phone. You can schedule in times for these activities in to your weekly timetable.
- *Utilise time that you waste*. Think about times of the day when you do nothing, such as waiting in queues, or commuting on the bus and train. The time can be used to do something.

Timetable

The timetable opposite can be used to plan your week.

Exams and revision

Exams are a common assessment method. They are used to test your understanding of course content and how you use it to discuss and evaluate issues. Thorough preparation for an exam is essential if you want to do well.

How to prepare for an exam

Below are tips to help you to plan your revision.

1   *Plan your time*. Revision should not be left to the last minute – begin early! You might have a lot of work to cover for different subjects, so you should plan your workload carefully. The time management techniques on the previous page will help you. For instance, you can create a revision timetable that includes the work you need to review, the study methods you will use, and any resources and support you need.

Time	Monday	Tuesday	Wednesday	Thursday	Friday	Saturday	Sunday
9:00							
10:00							
11:00							
12:00							
13:00							
14:00							
15:00							
16:00							
17:00							
18:00							
19:00							
20:00							
21:00							
22:00							

Remember to balance your revision with other activities such as regular meals, plenty of sleep, exercise, and relaxation.

2   *Select material to revise*. Organise your notes and decide on the material you need to cover. This will depend on the type of exam, what you already know, and suggestions from your tutor. Prioritise tasks according to the amount of time you have and the amount of material you need to remember.

3   *Study methods*. Think about different ways you can study. Have a go at using active learning techniques (see page 140) such as cards, studying with a friend, linking topics together, and predicting possible exam questions that could come up.

4   *Find out about the exam*. Read past exam papers to become familiar with the format of exam papers, including the types of questions, number of questions you need to answer and the allocation of marks. Also, check the arrangements of your exams (such as where the exam room and building is), and the items you are allowed to take into the exam room.

5   *Practise with a mock exam*. A mock exam is a practise exam that helps you to practise writing exam answers. The results of the mock exam might give you a good idea of how you will do in the real exam, and will give you the opportunity to practise.

6   *Relax!* Schedule-in a good night's sleep the night before an exam. Avoid stressful situations, such as arguments with your friends! See pages xx for tips about how to manage stress.

In the exam room

Plan your time and activities when you are in the exam room.

Read the exam instructions and questions very carefully. Read and understand a question before you answer it.

Use the first 5–10 minutes to read the questions and plan your answers (you might be able to use a page in the exam booklet to scribble an essay plan). Allocate some time at the end of the exam to re-read your answers to check for factual, grammatical and punctuation mistakes.

Don't leave the exam room early. Use any spare time to check your answers or to think about additional information to include.

> Your presentation and writing style is very important. Write clearly and use paragraphs.

> You may have a choice of questions to answer. Choose those that you have prepared for and can answer well. Answer the correct number of questions!

Problem solving

You will need to solve problems in your assignments and other course activities. The way to tackle a problem will depend on your course, the type and extent of the problem, and your personal preference. Below is a logical series of steps to help you think,

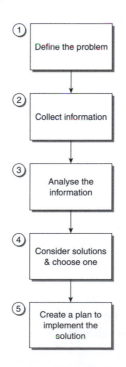

How to solve a problem

in general terms, about ways to find solutions. Every problem is different, so it is not necessary to follow each step, or in the order they are presented.

1   To develop a solution, you first need to understand and define the problem. Identify its different parts and how they are linked together. Thinking about these aspects will help you to know about what to solve, and the approaches you can take.
2   Collect information about the problem in order to learn more about it. The type and amount you need will depend on the problem, your resources, and the constraints of the project.
3   Critically evaluate the facts you have collected. You may also need to summarise the information or transform it into a different format (for example, via statistical analysis).
4   You should now be able to use the information you collected and analysed to suggest possible solutions. Think about what you want the solution to do. There may be more than one solution; if so, think about the strengths and weaknesses of each one.
5   After a solution has been chosen, go and apply it! If the problem is for an assignment, you could write it up in the form of an essay or report. Test the effectiveness of the solution – did it work? Can it be improved?

Independent and active learning

'Independent learning' means taking responsibility for your studies and relying on less direction from your teachers. Whereas your school teachers were primarily in charge of how you learnt, at university level you are expected to be more independent. You must decide how and when to study. The main benefit of independent learning is that you can pursue your learning in accordance with your own needs and preferences. Important attributes of an independent learner include:

- the ability to set clear targets
- good time-management skills
- the ability to identify your skills and seek ways to improve them
- relate classroom experiences with everyday life
- meet your classmates to share ideas and viewpoints.

'Active learning' emphasises 'learning by doing'. This means that instead of passively listening to a lecture, or reading a book, you should be engaged in the learning process. Active learning is, therefore, more interactive than traditional lectures. It helps learners to:

- retain more knowledge
- remember things for a longer time
- apply course content to a wider range of contexts
- enjoy the learning process.

Below are suggestions to help you to interact with, and use, your course materials:

- think about how different concepts covered in your course link together
- use course materials in a variety of ways
- critically analyse and evaluate your course content
- generate questions about your course materials and seek answers to them
- prepare for lectures
- study 'case studies' or visit local areas relevant to your course.

Critical thinking

At university level you are expected to think critically when listening to lectures, reading books, and writing assignments. Critical thinking involves considering the information provided or argument being made, and analysing whether there is sufficient evidence to support it. If you believe that an argument or conclusion is weak, then you are expected to challenge it and suggest alternatives. This approach may be very unlike what you were taught in school. At university, there will not always be right and wrong answers; many topics have contrasting viewpoints and arguments, and you are expected to weigh them up. In your assignments and exams, you will need to evaluate concepts and arguments, and judge how other people have done so.

Thinking critically:

- reduces the chances of a false premise
- improves the clarity and accuracy of content and reduces errors
- enables ideas to be developed further
- promotes fairness.

You should be constantly asking questions about your work. Critical thinking does not mean you should be criticising everything that you read and write! It does mean, however, that you should challenge any conclusions that seem weak. Below are ways to help you to think critically about information:

- Identify the argument, opinion or statement being made.
- Consider an issue very carefully and in detail. Take apart the pieces of an issue and see how they fit together.
- Do not rely on one view. Consider opinions from contrasting sides of an argument, including the evidence that supports each one.
- Evaluate evidence that is used to support an argument. Look for possible flaws.
- Is the information accurate and reliable? Was there any bias or unfairness? Is the evidence from a credible source?
- Try to understand how people arrive at their different arguments.
- Be flexible; consider alternative views, new ideas and be prepared to change your views.

Referencing and plagiarism

When you write an essay or report, you will need to read books, articles and other material to find information. These sources – known as references – should be listed in your work to show where the facts came from. As well as acknowledging other people's ideas, references also enhance the credibility of your writing, and enable the reader to access the material from which ideas come from.

When do I need to provide a reference?

Generally, any ideas or data that are not your own and are not common knowledge should be referenced in your work. This includes:

- a quotation (words that are copied exactly from another source)
- evidence you use to support your views
- a paraphrase (your own words to report other people's ideas)
- diagrams and other artwork
- data and statistical analysis (e.g., graphs, tables, etc)
- ideas that you have summarised to build a foundation for your argument
- controversial facts or opinions
- non-print sources such as the Internet, CD-ROMS, films, etc.

How to reference

The main way to reference information is to cite the source in the text; other people's ideas are briefly acknowledged in the main body of the text, and are detailed in a reference list and bibliography.

There are several referencing systems you can use to cite sources in your work. Each one provides a set of rules to follow. The system you should use depends on your discipline and course.

There are two main systems for sources cited in the text:

- *Author-date systems*. The author's surname and date of the publication are inserted into the text. Referencing systems that use this method include the Harvard system and APA system.
- *Numerical systems*. A small superscript number is inserted into the text instead of the author's surname. The references are then listed in numerical order in the reference list.

Your tutor or university library will be able to help you understand referencing styles.

Reference list and bibliography

All the references that you cite in your essay should be listed at the end in a 'reference list'. Other references that you used, but did not refer to, can be listed in a bibliography.

The references should be arranged alphabetically by the author's surname. Each reference should start on a separate line and separated by a space between each reference. If two or more references are written by the same author, they should be listed in order of their publication date. References by the same author that are published in the same year should be distinguished from each other by the letters a, b, c etc (e.g., Davey, 2005a; 2005b; 2005c).

There should be enough detail in each reference for the reader to find the source. The main points to include for each reference are:

- author's surname
- year of publication
- title of the article
- title, volume and issue number for journals, magazines, and newsletters
- page numbers
- place of publication (for a book)
- for an Internet source, the URL and the date you accessed it.

Tip

Don't leave the reference list until last! It is easier to write the references as you go along.

References must be correct, complete, and the listed in a consistent manner.

Plagiarism

Plagiarism is the use of other people's ideas and work without acknowledging them. It gives the impression that the work and ideas belong to the student and not the author. Plagiarism occurs when:

- other people's work or ideas are not referenced in essays and reports
- an assignment on one course is used as an assignment in another course (known as self-plagiarism)
- group members do not make an equal contribution to a task but claim they have
- an assignment is written by another person.

Plagiarism can either be intentional, when a person deliberately tries to pass other people's work as their own, or unintentional due to a lack of understanding. Both of the situations are regarded as serious offences in universities in the UK. Any student who plagiarises will face severe consequences, and could even be asked to withdraw from university. Make sure that you understand how to reference your work.

Reflective learning and assessing your skills

Reflective learning involves thinking about your previous learning experiences in order to improve how you can study in the future. The main aims of reflective learning are to:

- think about the way you study
- evaluate your progress on the course
- identify gaps in your skills and knowledge
- consider the factors that block your performance
- assess your strengths and weaknesses (SWOT analysis)
- develop a plan to improve your learning
- take responsibility for monitoring your progress.

Assessing your strengths and weaknesses

One way to look at your skills is to do a 'SWOT' analysis. SWOT is an acronym for:

- *Strengths*. The skills you are good at and can do.
- *Weaknesses*. The skills you are not good at.
- *Opportunities*. The benefits of learning new knowledge or skills.
- *Threats*. Possible problems that could get in the way of your studies.

Table 9.3 helps you to think and write about these four aspects.

Think about the way you learn

Begin by thinking, in general terms, about the way you study and your progress on the course. To gain further insight, you can think about specific experiences on your course. This can be done either in a structured way, such as writing a review of your experiences, or less formally by simply relaxing with a cup of coffee and thinking about your life as a student!

The questions below will help to guide your reflections about your learning experiences:

- How well are you doing on your course?
- How do you feel about the way that you did something (such as an essay)?
- What was good and not so good about the way you did it?

- If you do it again, what would you do differently?
- What improvements do you need to make?
- Have you experienced any problems on your course?

Other aspects to consider include your motivation, your attitudes to the course, and any factors blocking your learning. Each of these is important in your academic success.

SWOT analysis

Think about your experiences on the course, and the study skills. Write down your thoughts in the table below.	
STRENGTHS *Write down:* • *the things you are good at, and the skills you have* • *the strengths you have to aid the development of new skills*	**WEAKNESSES** *Write down:* • *the things you are not good at the skills you need to develop*
OPPORTUNITIES *Write down:* • *the benefits of studying your course and new skills* • *opportunities you have to learn*	**THREATS** *Write down:* • *the factors that get in your way when* • *you learn and develop new skills*

Analyse your strengths and weaknesses

Approaches to reflective learning

Below are other suggestions to help you to reflect.

- *Fill-in the self-evaluation form*. The next page describes how you can self-evaluate your ability at various study skills, and identify areas for improvement.
- *Write a reflective learning report*. Write an evaluation of your experiences on a course or specific event.
- *Keep a learning journal*. A diary or notebook can be used to record your on-going experiences. It can be completed weekly or several times a semester.
- *Portfolios*. You could be asked to compile a portfolio, which is a collection of work from your course. It can include assignments, examples of your assessed work and achievements, a log of your learning activities, learning plans, and evidence of your reflective learning
- *Critical incident analysis*. This method is used for work placements and professional training. It is a record of events you experience during your work. It includes a description of the event, how the situation was managed, and suggestions for improvement.
- *Feedback*. Views from teachers and other people about your work is very helpful and will give you evidence of your strengths and weaknesses. Look at your tutors' comments on your previous assignments.

Reflective learning is becoming popular as an assessed piece of work. You may be asked to write about experiences on your course, work placement, field courses, etc.

Table 9.4   How good am I at study skills?

You can use the table below to self-assess your current ability of each study skill. Give the reasons for your choice. Try to judge your skills accurately – don't put yourself down, or over-rate yourself!

Study skill	Your current skill level	Evidence of your skill level	Need for improvement
	Rate your ability of each skill using a scale of 1–4 (1 = low ability; 4 = high ability)	Give examples of when you used each skill, and how you developed it	Rate your need to improve each skill using a scale of 1–4 (1 = little need to improve; 4 = big need to improve)
Essay writing			
Report writing			
Oral presentation			
Critical thinking			

Which skills do I need to develop?

Below is a table for you to complete. It helps you to record your strengths and weaknesses with regards to specific study skills. Try to complete the questionnaire regularly (for example, every six months), to update your record of your skills. This will enable you to monitor your progress.

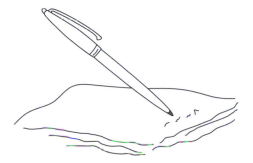

Developing your skills

Table 9.5 should help you to identify the skills you need to improve. You are now in a position to find ways to develop your skills. You could focus on the skills that are required by your course. For example, some courses use exams as an

Table 9.5

Study skill	Your current skill level	Evidence of your skill level	Need for improvement
Creative thinking			
Forming arguments			
Exam and revision techniques			
Note taking			
Problem solving			
Time-management			
Reflective learning			
Independent learning			
Self-motivation			
Academic English			
Critical thinking			

assessment method, whereas others do not, and this may influence whether or not you should spend time learning about examination and revision techniques. Also think about the skills you would like to develop for a future job and career after you graduate.

You will practise and develop your skills as your course progresses. Pay attention to feedback about your work from your tutors and classmates. Other sources of help include:

- books about study skills
- tutors
- study skills advisors
- university library
- a mentor.

Attending university is not the only way to develop skills. Other avenues include part-time or voluntary work, playing sports, involvement in committees, and social activities.

Creating a development plan

A development plan will help to guide how you can develop your skills. Table 9.6 is a blank learning plan for you to fill in. It includes details about:

- *Your goals*. A goal is a clear statement about the study skill you want to develop, and the level of ability you want to achieve.
- *Action needed to reach your goals*. A description of the activities you need to do, and how long it will take to develop your skills. You are likely to make progress if you break down the goals into small steps and then identify the tasks needed for each one.
- *Resources and support*. Help that is available to help you reach your goals.
- *Constraints*. Circumstances that stop you from meeting your goals. Examples of constraints are time, uncertainty, no opportunities, or lack of motivation.
- *Timescale*. The time you need to achieve your goal.

After you have created your plan, make sure you use it! Put it on your wall so that it reminds you of what you need to do. Review and update your plan regularly depending on how you progress with it. After you reach your goals, you can set new or more challenging ones. Conversely, if you cannot meet your goals in the timescale set, you can either extend the timescale, or examine whether or not the goals need to be amended.

Table 9.6   A plan to improve your study skills

My goals	Action needed to reach my goals	Resources available	Constraints	Time scale
LONG TERM				
SHORT TERM				

10 Life after graduation

INTRODUCTION

After reading this chapter, you should be able to:

☑ Consider the options available after graduation
☑ Choose a career, and develop a career plan
☑ Search and apply for jobs
☑ Write a CV and prepare for job interviews

What will you do after your course finishes? This chapter discusses your options, and helps you to prepare for graduate life. There is information about postgraduate study, graduate jobs, and career planning. There is also advice about how to write a CV, look for jobs, and prepare to leave the UK.

What are the options?

The options open to you after graduation should be considered very carefully to ensure that you make the best choice. Early planning is essential because courses, graduate jobs, and scholarships have closing dates. Be flexible in your thinking; there are many opportunities, and each one has pros, cons and long-term implications. Your options include:

- further (postgraduate) study
- a graduate career
- work experience
- a year out or voluntary work
- setting up a business.

There are several things you can do to prepare for life after graduation:

- Explore postgraduate courses and their entry requirements, as well as scholarships and other financial support programmes.
- If you're thinking about undertaking a research degree, contact potential supervisors for advice.
- Find out about careers and jobs that interest you. Contact graduate employers for details of their recruitment schemes.
- Gain work experience while you are a student, e.g., during the summer vacations.
- Write your CV and assess your skills and interests in relation to career options.
- If applicable, find out about how to extend your visa. Advice about how to do this is available from the Home Office (Border and Immigration Agency) or the Immigration Advisory Service.

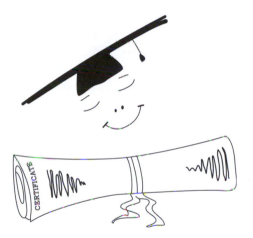

Further study

You may be thinking about continuing your studies through a postgraduate or other course. A postgraduate course will enable you to:

- study a subject in detail
- learn a new subject that will open up an alternative career path
- improve your skills
- obtain a professional qualification.

There are a wide variety of postgraduate courses on offer. Courses characteristics vary: you will need to weigh up factors such as their content; taught or research programmes; type of university, fees and funding; and whether it can be studied on a full- or part-time basis. See Chapter 1 for advice about choosing a suitable course.

Staying and working in the UK

You may be eager to enter the world of work! One option is to return to your country to find a job. Alternatively, it may be possible for some students to work in the UK. There are restrictions for most international students who want to live and work in the UK (the situation is different, however, for students from EEA countries, who have few restrictions). Immigration rules applicable to certain students make it clear that they should intend to return to their country after they complete their studies. However, some students find that they are able to stay after graduation. For example, there are schemes that allow non-EEA students to stay after their studies; information is available from the Home Office (Border and Immigration Agency). Be aware that the rules change regularly and there are closing dates for applications.

Graduate jobs

Many jobs and careers are open only to graduates, and are known as 'graduate jobs'. They are more senior and offer a higher salary than non-graduate jobs. There are three main ways to get into the graduate job market:

- *Direct entry*. Involves applying for a specific job and starting as soon as you join the company.
- *Graduate recruitment or training schemes* (see below).
- *A professional training course*. Qualifies students for certain professions or increases their chances of finding a job.

What is a graduate recruitment scheme?

Many large companies have recruitment schemes specifically for graduates. They are intensive development programmes that prepare new employees for senior positions. Training lasts between one and two years, and may involve placements in different areas of the company.

Closing dates can be as early as the autumn before graduation. Selection procedures can be tough and involve interviews, assessment days, and psychometric tests. There are several ways to find out about graduate recruitment schemes: contact individual companies for details about their schemes; search for vacancies at career websites such as Prospects; look in the university career's centre; or visit a Careers Fair.

How do I choose a career?

You may – or may not – have decided the type of career you would like to pursue after graduation. Finding a suitable career is a multi-step process: it requires understanding your skills and personal qualities, matching them with the characteristics of various jobs, and then developing a plan to achieve what you want. These steps are summarised below.

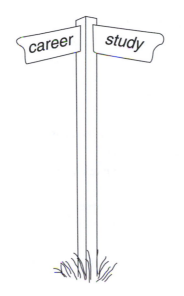

Step 1: Understand yourself

Think about yourself – your interests, skills, abilities, personality, and personal values that motivate you. This is important because your personal attributes play a role in determining the types of jobs you can do and will enjoy. Ask yourself:

- What do I want from a job/career?
- What am I able to do?
- What do I enjoy doing?
- What makes me happy?
- Is money or job satisfaction more important to me?
- Are there any new skills or knowledge that I want to learn?

Identifying skills and abilities is not easy. The SWOT analysis in Chapter 9 is a good starting point. Also, there are various tools available from your university's career's centre to help provide an objective assessment. They include the 'Prospects Planner' on the Prospects website, which is an online tool to help university students and graduates to explore how their interests and skills relate to various career areas. Bear in mind, however, that self-assessment tools can only give suggestions – they cannot tell you what to do!

Other factors to think about include the lifestyle you want, your preferred working environment (e.g., hours, pay, and conditions), and the needs and opinions of your family.

Step 2: Find out about careers and employers

After you have assessed your interests and skills, the next stage is to match them to suitable careers. To do this, search for details about different jobs, talk to careers advisors, attend a Careers Fair, and contact employers. Find out information about:

- a range of jobs and employers
- careers related to your course
- employment areas that are open to any graduate
- opportunities to gain work experience
- your eligibility to work in the UK (it can restrict the type of work you can do).

After you have selected a few possible careers, investigate them further to see if they are right for you. Find out what each one entails, the skills required, and the working conditions and typical salary.

A good way to learn more about a job is to talk to people who are already doing it. Possible questions to ask are:

- What activities do you do in a typical day?
- What do you like and dislike about the job?
- Do you have any advice to help me find a similar job?

Step 3: Make your career decisions

The next step is to evaluate the information you have collected about different careers to narrow the options down. Jobs can be prioritised in order of your preference based on how they relate to your enjoyment, skills and preferences. Making a choice will be difficult; take your time, as it could have a lasting impact on your life!

Step 4: Create a career plan

It is useful to develop a plan that lists all the steps you need to take to reach your desired job. The steps can be listed on the plan as 'goals', accompanied by a list of the activities and time needed to accomplish them. To help you think about them, a blank learning plan is provided for you on page 156. The plan helps you to focus on three main questions:

- *Where am I now?* Summarise your current situation, including your qualifications, skills, and work experience.
- *Where do I want to be?* Compare your current situation with your chosen one.
- *How can I get there?* Focus on the things you need to do to reach your goals. If you are at the end of your course, your plan could include a resumé and a job search strategy. Students at earlier stages can explore options such as gaining experience through internships, volunteering, and part-time jobs.

Your plan will depend on if you have identified a specific career, or whether you only have a general idea about what you want to do. For example, if your career goal is to become a teacher, then you will probably need to get further training and teaching experience.

> **Tip**
>
> Be flexible and patient during your career planning. In the UK, graduates are not restricted to jobs related to their degree subject. Also, it is common for people to change their careers several times during their working lives.

Ensure that your goals, timescales and deadlines are realistic. Also make a note of the possible obstacles that could prevent you from reaching goals, and think of ways to deal with them.

It is worthwhile devising several plans in case your first choice does not work out. Be flexible – you can change your mind along the way, and plans can be amended over time as goals and priorities change.

Gaining work experience

Employers prefer graduates who have work experience as well as academic qualifications. Work experience helps to develop transferable skills and therefore increases employability. There are several ways you can obtain work experience:

- *Internship.* A supervised work placement in a company, often during the summer vacation or a semester.
- *Summer employment.* Many students work during the summer. The job may not necessarily be related to the degree subject.
- *Volunteering and community work.* Charities, community groups, and other organisations welcome volunteers to help with their activities.
- *Gap year.* A period of time (often a year) spent away from university in order to gain work or other experience.
- *Sandwich course.* A period of employment that is part of a degree course.

- *Work shadowing*. Observing staff at work in order to understand their job.
- *Extra-curricular activities*. Duties related to student life but are not part of a course (e.g., being a committee member, student representative, or working in the Student Union).

Table 10.1   Career plan

Goals	Action needed to reach goals	Time scale
LONG TERM		
SHORT TERM		

How do I find a job?

Finding a job is not always easy; it takes time and requires patience and good organisational skills. The job hunting process can be considered a job in itself! There are a number of places where you can look for a job:

- *Job advertisements*. Jobs are advertised in local, regional and national newspapers; trade magazines; and the local job centre.
- *Milk round*. A milk round is a graduate Career Fair, held at universities, in which large organisations advertise their positions and recruit students.
- *Friends, family, and networking*. Not all jobs are advertised; try to find them from people you know. Ask other graduates how they found their jobs.
- *Recruitment agencies*. Companies that help employers find staff. They advertise permanent and temporary jobs.
- *University careers office and job shop*. Many universities have a careers office or job centre that advertises jobs and graduate recruitment schemes. They will have details about international and national opportunities.
- *Internet*. There are many online websites that advertise jobs. Websites of individual companies list their openings.
- *Speculative applications*. It is possible to find a job by sending your CV and a covering letter to companies to enquire if they have any vacancies.

Before searching for a job, remember to check your visa status and immigration conditions.

Job hunting tips...

There are several things you can do to maximise the success of your job search

Prepare for your job search

- Understand your skills and how they relate to different jobs
- Identify jobs that interest you, and research them in detail
- Visit the university's career's centre and use their facilities
- Write a good CV and covering letter
- Research different companies

Search for a job

- Be prepared to spend time searching for jobs
- Be realistic about what you can do
- Attend a Careers Fair
- Consider seeking help from a recruitment agency
- Network with people who can assist you to find a job

After your job search

- Follow up job applications or discussions with employers
- Keep people informed of your job search
- Ask for feedback about unsuccessful interviews
- Keep up your motivation; seek support from your family and friends
- Practise job interview skills

How to write your CV and covering letter

What is a CV?

A Curriculum Vitae (CV) is a document that outlines your qualifications, experiences and skills, and how they relate to the job you are applying for. It is likely to be the first piece of information about you that a future employer sees. It should provide them with enough detail to judge your suitability for the job.

What should I include in my CV?

There is no best or universally accepted way to write a CV. It depends on the type of job you are applying for and your personal preference. Even so, most CV's contain the following details:

(Continued)

- *Personal details.* The first section includes your contact details (e.g., name, address, telephone number, etc).
- *Career aim.* Some job applicants like to write a brief statement that summarises their career skills and aspirations.
- *Career and skills summary.* List details about your employment history. Begin with the most recent job. Include the job title, company name, and a list of the main responsibilities and achievements.
- *Education and qualifications.* Write about your degree and other qualifications. Include the name of your degree, the university, graduation date, grades, and course details. If you received a qualification overseas, note its equivalence to a UK qualification.
- *Interests and achievements.* Write down your hobbies. Emphasise activities that utilise the skills that are needed for the job you are applying for. Also list additional skills such as a driving licence, languages you can speak, and computer skills.
- *Details of referees.* Note the contact details of referees, or write 'references available on request'. Employers usually prefer one reference from your tutor and another from your previous or current employer. Obviously, choose a referee who will support your application.

A CV should be written to show that you are the best person for the job. Remember to highlight your skills and achievements, and don't put yourself down!

Different types of CVs

There are three common CV formats:

- *Chronological CV.* A traditional format that outlines your career history, education, etc. It is used when applying for a job directly related to your current or previous one.
- *Skills-based CV.* Uses evidence from your work experience to highlight your skills. It can be used to show skills that you developed in the past, or when your previous job was not relevant to the job you are applying for.
- *Creative CV.* This format has no set style, and can use creative designs such as different colours, fonts, or structure. Some applicants use this format when applying for creative jobs in advertising and PR, but it is not a common format and some employers do not like it.

There are also other CV formats that may be used for jobs related to law, academia, and scientific and technological jobs. Further information about them is available from your university careers service.

When should I use my CV?

A CV should be used when:

- a company requests it
- the application method is not specified
- your application is speculative (that is, if you are writing to an employer who has not advertised a position).

It is also useful to take your CV to recruitment and careers fairs to show employers. Bear in mind, however, that some companies do not like CVs, and instead ask applicants to complete application forms.

If you are applying for more than one job, tailor the CV to each one. In order to make your CV relevant, consider the following questions:

- What activities does the job involve?
- What skills and experiences are needed?
- Which CV format is suitable?

The covering letter

A CV is usually accompanied by a covering letter, which introduces you and encourages the employer to read your CV. The following points can be included:

- an introduction
- reference to the job you are applying for
- a summary of your suitability for the job
- a list of your skills (link them to the job criteria).

You can also use the covering letter to express your enthusiasm and commitment for the job, explain what attracts you to it, and explain any special circumstances or a particular aspect of your application.

What about the content, length, and presentation?

Take care when writing a CV:

- Write clearly and concisely. Use action words (see next page).
- Be honest and factual, and leave out irrelevant or negative information.
- Use bullet points to summarise points.
- Ensure that the CV and covering letter are not too long. A CV is generally no more than 2 pages (a one-page CV is becoming popular).
- Ask a native English speaker to check your grammar and spelling.
- Use a consistent style throughout (font, spacing, margins, paragraphs, etc).
- Use good quality paper. Type the CV; use standard typeface, and black ink on white paper.

(Continued)

Action words

'Action words' are keywords (usually verbs) that you can use in your CV to emphasise your achievements and abilities. They include:

achieved	experience	planned
administered	facilitated	positive
analysed	guided	prepared
competent	implemented	operated
communicated	improved	proficient
co-ordinated	initiated	represented
created	led	resourceful
designed	managed	specialised
developed	monitored	successful
directed	organised	supported
effective	participated	supervised
established	performed	trained

Successful job interviews

After considering your CV, an employer might want to interview you. The interview also gives you an opportunity to find out more about the job.

Types of interviews and questions

There are different types of interviews. They can take place via a telephone conversation, one-to-one meeting, panel interview in which several people conduct the interview, or a work-based assessment in which the candidate is assessed while doing the job. They can take place in the company, assessment centres, or in less formal settings.

How do I prepare for an interview?

Good preparation is essential.

- Know what the employer is looking for. Read the job advert to identify the skills required.
- Review your course materials, particularly those relevant to the job, as employers may want to ask you about them.

- Research the employer and the job. You will be expected to show awareness of their organisation. Information is available from the employer's website, people who work there, and your university's career's service.
- Plan how you will get to the interview. Take a map with you!
- Consider possible questions that interviewers could ask, and plan good answers to them. Think of several questions you can ask the employer.
- Practise your interview skills. Ask your career's advisor for help.
- Try to relax!

During the interview

- Dress appropriately (conservatively and smartly). Wear clean and ironed clothes.
- Plan to arrive 10–15 minutes early.
- Be polite and friendly to everyone, including the receptionist or assistant.
- Pay attention to body language and facial expressions. Although you may be nervous, try to smile, and look friendly and approachable. Sit up straight, and listen attentively. Remain calm, and avoid any nervous habits.
- Take necessary documents to the interview, such as references, certificates of your qualifications, and examples of your work.

Interview questions

Interviewers could ask a range of questions. They might ask you to provide more detail about the points raised in your CV, or ask competency-based questions that focus on the skills needed for the job. For example, you could be asked to provide evidence by describing your past experiences about how your skills and experience relate to the job you are applying for. The interviewers could test how you respond to certain situations. If you are applying for a technical or specialist position, the questions could test your knowledge.

Below are some common interview questions:

- Can you tell me more about yourself?
- Why do you want to work in this company?
- What are your strengths and weaknesses?
- What goals have you established in your career?
- What motivates you?
- Where do you want to be in 5 years?
- Can you explain this gap in your employment history?
- Can you give any examples about how you achieve a challenging goal?

These questions are only a few examples. Further help about dealing with job interviews is available from the university's career's centre and from books available in your library.

After the interview

- Think about the strong and weak points of your interview performance, and ways to improve next time.
- Consider writing a 'thank you' letter or email to the interviewers.
- If you do not hear from the interviewer in the time they stated, call them to enquire about the status of your application.
- If you are unsuccessful, do not take rejection personally. Jobs are competitive and attract applications from excellent people. Ask for feedback about your performance in the interview.

Starting your own business

Another option after you graduate is to set up a business, either in the UK or your country. You should check the immigration conditions that apply to you, as there may be restrictions. There are good reasons to consider self-employment. They include:

- an opportunity to do what you are interested in
- being your own boss; control over your own working conditions
- the challenge of setting up and running a business (personal satisfaction)
- an opportunity to make lots of money
- you have a unique business idea that can be successful.

Your business could be related to your degree subject or experience, an interest or hobby you wish to develop, or a gap in the market. It could be set up from scratch, or by buying an existing business or franchise.

The decision to set up a business should not be taken lightly. At the very least, you should have:

- a well developed business plan
- a location for the business
- a market for your products and services
- financial support
- business awareness, including skills in marketing, financial planning, awareness of competitors, etc
- the right skills, attributes and personality to be a successful entrepreneur.

If you are interested in setting up a business, you will need to thoroughly research the situation. Aspects to consider include business planning, marketing and market research, taxation, forming and naming your business, and choosing and maintaining the workplace. There are many resources to help you, including reference books and leaflets available from your university's career's office or local library, websites (e.g., Business Link), organisations such as The Federation of Small Businesses, and banks (major high street banks provide booklets about setting up a business).

Preparing to leave the UK

After you finish your studies, you will need to plan to return to your country. There are several things to do before leaving.

Travel arrangements

Book travel arrangements to your country. Tickets booked in advance are usually cheaper.

Think about how you will send your belongings home. The baggage allowance on the plane will be limited; if you have many items to take, send them via shipping freight or air cargo. Sell your unwanted belongings and old textbooks – put adverts on university notice boards around the university, in the local newspaper, or donate items to a charity shop.

Find out about customs regulations. Do you have any items that are not allowed in to your country? Will you be charged customs' duties on any of your goods? You may want to buy memorabilia to remind you of your enjoyable time at university and in the UK.

Your forwarding address

Tell others that you are leaving, and give them your new address. Inform your university, alumni, department, previous landlord, bank, employer, utility companies, doctor, and police. You can ask friends to forward your letters to you, or arrange for a re-direction service from the Post Office.

Before you leave the UK, ensure that you have paid any outstanding bills, fees, or overdrafts. Give plenty of notice to your landlord, and ensure that the tenancy contract has been completed; remember to ask for your deposit to be returned!

Tax

You may be entitled to Income Tax refunds if you have worked and paid Income Tax. You may be able to claim Value Added Tax (VAT) if you have recently bought items (e.g., large electrical items) in the UK and have taken them back to a country outside the EU.

References

Visit your university's career centre. They will be able to give advice about careers, and can help you identify employers and apply for jobs in your country. Ask your tutors or current employer to write references for you to take to future job interviews.

Reverse culture shock

Just like when you moved to the UK, you might experience difficulties settling in to your former routines and habits when you return home. This problem is known as 'reverse culture shock' and is common, especially among students who have adjusted particularly well to British culture. You may have noticed that your lifestyle, attitudes, and habits changed somewhat to fit in with your student life in the UK. It may be necessary to adjust again when you return home. See Chapter 2 to learn more about culture shock and how to deal with it. Remember to stay connected with the UK; for example, you can join the university's alumni association (a service for former students) and get involved in cultural programmes in your country about the UK.

Before you leave the UK ...

There are several things to do before you leave the UK

☐   Plan your journey and book the tickets

☐   Ensure that your visa is valid during the time you stay in the UK

☐   Check the customs regulations in your country

☐   Contact the airline to check the baggage allowance

☐   Send your belongings home via shipping freight or air cargo

☐   Sell unwanted belongings or donate them to a charity shop

☐   Notify others about your departure and new address

☐   Enquire about your eligibility for Income Tax and VAT refunds

☐   Pay any outstanding bills, fees, and overdraft

☐   Visit the university's career centre

☐   Obtain references from your tutors or employer

☐   Exchange contact details with your friends!

☐   Give notice to your landlord, and ask for the deposit to be refunded

☐   Prepare for 'reverse culture shock'!

Glossary

Academic English   Advanced English used in university. Academic English is formal, concise, impersonal and objective.

Academic year   The time period every year from the beginning to the end of your studies. Usually begins in September or October and ends in June or July.

British Council   A UK organisation (with offices around the world) that provides information about UK educational opportunities.

Careers Fair   An event in which employers give information about jobs and careers in their companies.

Clearing   A service offered by UCAS in August and September which allows students who do not have a university place to apply for vacancies.

College of Further Education   Mainly provides courses for students up to the age of 18, although may offer courses such as HNDs and Foundation degrees.

Council tax   A property tax that tenants should pay to the local council to contribute towards public services.

Course fee   Covers the cost of the teaching and course materials you will receive, as well as exams, assessment, and learning facilities.

Credit   Each module has a credit rating which indicates the amount of learning that takes place.

Credit transfer   The transfer of credits awarded for a previous course to a qualification you want to study in the UK.

Deposit   Money paid to a landlord to cover any damage that could be caused during the tenancy or non-payment of rent.

Distance learning   Courses that can be studied without attending class; there is no or little requirement to be present in the classroom.

European Economic Area (EEA)   Consists of EU countries, Iceland, Liechtenstein and Norway. Swiss nationals have similar rights to EEA nationals.

Entry requirements   The requirements needed to study a course; can include qualifications, exam scores, English language ability, etc.

Freshers' Fair   A programme of social events at the beginning of term to find out about student clubs and societies.

Graduate recruitment scheme   A development programme in a job that prepares graduates for senior positions in a company.

GP   A local medical doctor. Provides advice and diagnosis on a range of health problems, and gives treatment and prescriptions.

Halls of residence   A student dormitory. Includes a single room, bed, wardrobe, desk, and a shared or private bathroom and kitchen.

Hardship fund   Financial help from a university for students with unexpected and unforeseen financial problems.

Highway Code   A set of rules that apply to all road users.

International English Language Testing System (IELTS)   An English language test to assess whether non-native English speakers have sufficient English skills to succeed at university.

League table   An unofficial list of universities based on their performance with regards teaching, research, and student support.

LGBT   A support group for lesbian, gay, bisexual, and transgender students.

Meningitis   A dangerous disease that causes inflammation of the lining of the brain.

Module   Courses are 'modular'. This means that they are divided into self-contained units of study known as 'modules'.

The National Health Service (NHS)   The UK's government-funded health care system.

Prescription medicine   Medicine that can only be obtained with a prescription (permission from a doctor).

Nightline   A telephone or email service run by trained students that provides information and support for other students.

Overseas fee   Tuition fee for students from outside the EEA.

Professor   A senior teacher and researcher who is recognised for their scholarly achievements.

Senate   A governing body that directs university policies and academic quality. Other committees include the Court and Council.

Scholarship Financial support for students. Some cover all tuition and living expenses, whereas others offer a smaller contribution.

Socrates-Erasmus A scheme that enables European students to study in the UK (or in another European country).

Student Union An organisation that provides advice to students, and provides facilities for social and organisational activities.

SWOT A tool to assess the strengths, weaknesses, opportunities and threats of a given situation.

Vocational course A course that teaches skills for a specific career or job, in contrast to academic courses that are not linked to any specific job.

Vice-Chancellor The leader of a university. Also known as a President, Principal, or Chairperson.

Visa Permission from the British Government to enter the UK.

Yellow pages A telephone directory that lists businesses, organisations, services, and products. They are listed alphabetically.

Below is a list of abbreviations of academic degrees

UNDERGRADUATE QUALIFICATIONS

CertHE	Certificate of Higher Education
HND	Higher National Diploma
FdA, FdEd, FdEng, FdBus, FdSc, FdTech	Foundation Degree
BA	Bachelor of Arts
BBus	Bachelor of Business
BSc	Bachelor of Science
BArch	Bachelor of Architecture
BEng	Bachelor of Engineering
BCom	Bachelor of Commerce
BCS	Bachelor of Computer Science
BEc	Bachelor of Economics
BFA	Bachelor of Fine Arts
BMath	Bachelor of Mathematics
BMus	Bachelor of Music
BPharm	Bachelor of Pharmacy
BTech	Bachelor of Technology
BSocSci	Bachelor of Social Science
LLB	Bachelor of Law

POSTGRADUATE QUALIFICATIONS

PGCert	Postgraduate Certificate
PGDip	Postgraduate Diploma
PGCE	Postgraduate Certificate of Education
MA	Master of Arts
MBio	Master of Biology
MSc	Master of Science
MEd	Master of Education
MEng	Master of Engineering
MPhil	Master of Philosophy
MRes	Master of Research
MBA	Master of Business Administration
MDiv	Master of Divinity
MLitt	Master of Letters
MPH	Master of Public Health
MMus	Master of Music
LLM	Master of Law

DOCTORATES

PhD (DPhil)	Doctor of Philosophy
e.g., DClinPsy, EdD, DBA	Professional doctorates

Directory

Below is a list of organisations and government departments that you can contact for information about the topics mentioned in this guide. Note that some organisations have offices throughout the UK and overseas; therefore, you can visit their website to locate the nearest one. Look in the telephone directory or on the Internet for details of other organisations to contact.

Alcoholics Anonymous
General Service Office
PO Box 1
10 Toft Green
York YO1 7ND
0845 769 7555
www.alcoholics-anonymous.org.uk

Border and Immigration Agency (Home Office)
www.ind.homeoffice.gov.uk
www.workingintheuk.gov.uk
www.ukvisas.gov.uk

British Council
10 Spring Gardens
London SW1A 2BN
0161 957 7755
www.britishcouncil.org

Buckingham Palace
www.royal.gov.uk (the official web site of the British Monarchy)

Business Link
0845 600 9 006
www.businesslink.gov.uk

Childcare Link
Opportunity Links
Trust Court
Vision Park
Histon
Cambridge CB4 9PW
08000 96 02 96
www.childcarelink.gov.uk

Chip and Pin
www.chipandpin.co.uk

Citizen's Advice Bureau
115-123 Pentonville Road
London N1 9LZ
020 7833 2181
www.citizensadvice.org.uk

Daycare Trust
21 St George's Road
London SE1 6ES
020 7840 3350
www.daycaretrust.org.uk

Department for Education and Skills (DfES)
Sanctuary Buildings
Great Smith Street
London SW1P 3BT
0870 000 2288
www.dfes.gov.uk

Department of Health
Richmond House
79 Whitehall
London SW1A 2NS
020 7210 4850
www.dh.gov.uk

Department for Work and Pensions
www.dwp.gov.uk

Driver and Vehicle Licensing Agency (DVLA)
Swansea SA6 7JL
Tel: 0870 240 0009
www.dvla.gov.uk

Driver and Vehicle Licensing Northern Ireland (DVLNI)
Castlerock Road
Coleraine
Co. Londonderry BT51 3TB
0845 402 4000
www.dvlni.gov.uk

Financial Times League Table (www.ft.com)

Foreign and Commonwealth Office
King Charles Street
London SW1A 2AH
020 7008 1500
www.fco.gov.uk

The Higher Education Statistics Agency
95 Promenade
Cheltenham
GL50 1HZ
01242 255577
www.hesa.ac.uk

Graduate Teacher Training Registry (GTTR)
Rosehill
New Barn Lane
Cheltenham
Gloucestershire
GL52 3LZ
0870 1122205
www.gttr.ac.uk

Highway Code
www.highwaycode.gov.uk

HM Revenue and Customs
www.hmrc.gov.uk

Houses of Parliament
www.parliament.uk

IELTS
www.ielts.org

Immigration Advisory Service
3rd Floor, County House
190 Great Dover Street
London SE1 4YB
020 7967 1200
www.iasuk.org

London Cycling Campaign
www.lcc.org.uk

Meningitis Trust
Fern House
Bath Road
Stroud
Gloucestershire GL5 3TJ
0800 028 18 28
www.meningitis-trust.org

Meningitis Research Foundation
Midland Way
Thornbury
Bristol BS35 2BS
080 8800 3344
www.meningitis.org

National Academic Recognition Information Centre
Oriel House
Oriel Road
Cheltenham
GL50 1XP
0870 9904 088
www.naric.org.uk

National Cycle Network Centre
Sustrans offices
2 Cathedral Square
College Green
Bristol
BS1 5DD
0117 926 8893
www.sustrans.org.uk

National Drugs Helpline (also called 'Talk To Frank')
0800 77 66 00
www.talktofrank.com

National Express Limited
Ensign Court
4 Vicarage Road
Edgbaston
Birmingham B15 3ES
08705 808080
www.nationalexpress.com

National Union of Students (NUS)
Snape Road

Macclesfield
Cheshire SK10 2NZ
0845 045 1069
www.nusonline.co.uk

Mind
15-19 Broadway
London E15 4BQ
0845 766 0163
www.mind.org.uk

National Rail Enquiries
08457 48 49 50
www.nationalrail.co.uk

National Health Service (NHS)
The Department of Health
Richmond House
79 Whitehall
London SW1A 2NL
0207 210 4850
www.nhs.uk

NHS Direct
7th Floor
207 Old Street
London EC1V 9NR
0845 4647
www.nhsdirect.nhs.uk

Ofstead
Royal Exchange Buildings
St Ann's Square
Manchester M2 7LA
08456 404040
www.ofsted.gov.uk

Overseas Visitors Records Office
Brandon House
180 Borough High Street
London SE1 1LH
020 7230 1208

Post Office
Freepost
PO BOX 740
Brampton
Barnsley S73 0UF
08457 22 33 44
www.postoffice.co.uk

Prospects
Prospects House
Booth Street East
Manchester M13 9EP
0161 277 5200
www.prospects.ac.uk

Quality Assurance Agency
Southgate House
Southgate Street

Gloucester GL1 1UB
01452 557000
www.qaa.ac.uk

Research Assessment Exercise (RAE)
Northavon House
Coldharbour Lane
Bristol BS16 1QD
0117 931 7185
www.rae.ac.uk

RAC Motoring Services
Great Park Road
Bradley Stoke
Bristol BS32 4QN
08705 722 722
www.rac.co.uk

Socrates-Erasmums
British Council
10 Spring Gardens
London
SW1A 2BN
020 7389 4910
0207 389 4426
www.erasmus.ac.uk

Samaritans
PO Box 90 90
Stirling FK8 2SA
08457 90 90 90

The Daily Telegraph University league table
www.telegraph.co.uk/education

The Good University Guide
www.thetimes.co.uk/education

The Guardian University guide
education.guardian.co.uk

The National Federation of Self-Employed and Small Businesses Ltd (FSB)
Sir Frank Whittle Way
Blackpool Business Park
Blackpool FY4 2FE 01253 336000
www.fsb.org.uk

The Sunday Times Good University Guide
www.thetimes.co.uk/education

The TrainLine
PO BOX 222333
Edinburgh EH11 3AF
www.thetrainline.com

The Teaching Quality Information survey
www.tqi.ac.uk

Times Higher Student Satisfaction Rating
www.thes.co.uk

Traveline
www.traveline.org.uk
www.samaritans.org.uk

UKCOSA: The Council for International Education
9-17 St Albans Place
London N1 0NX
020 7288 4330
www.ukcosa.org.uk

Universities and Colleges Admissions Service (UCAS)
Rosehill
New Barn Lane
Cheltenham
Gloucestershire GL52 3LZ
0870 1122211
www.ucas.ac.uk

UKvisas
Foreign and Commonwealth Office
King Charles Street
London SW1A 2AH
0845 010 5555
www.ukvisas.gov.uk

VisitBritain
Thames Tower
Blacks Road
London W6 9EL
0208846 9000
www.visitbritain.com

Below is a list of universities and colleges that you can contact for information about their higher education courses.

Aberdeen University
King's College
Aberdeen AB24 3FX
www.abdn.ac.uk
01224 273504

Abertay Dundee University
Bell Street
Dundee
DD1 1HG
www.abertay.ac.uk
01382 308080

Aberystwyth (University of Wales)
Old College
King Street
Aberystwyth
SY23 2AX
www.aber.ac.uk
01970 622021

Anglia Ruskin University
Bishop Hall Lane

Chelmsford
Essex
CM1 1SQ
www.anglia.ac.uk
0845 271 3333

Arts Institute at Bournemouth
Wallisdown
Poole
BH12 5HH
www.aib.ac.uk
01202 363225

Askham Bryan College
Askham Bryan
York
YO23 3FR
www.askham-bryan.ac.uk
01904 772211

Aston University
Aston Triangle
Birmingham
B4 7ET

www.aston.ac.uk
0121 204 4444

Bangor (University of Wales)
Bangor
Gwynedd
LL57 2DG
www.bangor.ac.uk
01248 382016/2017

Barking College
Dagenham Road
Romford
Essex
RM7 0XU
www.barkingcollege.ac.uk
01708 770000

Barony College
Parkgate
Dumfries
DG1 3NE
www.barony.ac.uk
01387 860251

Basingstoke College of
Technology
Basingstoke
RG21 8TN
www.bcot.ac.uk
01256 354141

Bath University
Claverton Down
Bath
BA2 7AY
www.bath.ac.uk
01225 383019

Bath Spa University
Newton Park
Newton St Loe
Bath
BA2 9BN
www.bathspa.ac.uk
01225 875875

Bedford College
Cauldwell Street
Bedford
MK42 9AH
www.bedford.ac.uk
01234 291000

Bedfordshire University
Park Square
Luton
LU1 3JU
www.beds.ac.uk
01582 489286

Bell College
Hamilton
Lanarkshire
ML3 0JB
www.bell.ac.uk
01698 283100

Birmingham College of Food,
Tourism & Creative Studies
Summer Row
Birmingham
B3 1JB
www.bcftcs.ac.uk
0121 604 1040

Birmingham University
Edgbaston

Birmingham
B15 2TT
www.bham.ac.uk
0121 4158900

Bishop Burton College
Bishop Burton
Beverley
East Yorkshire
HU17 8QG
www.bishopburton.ac.uk
01964 553000

Bishop Grosseteste University
College
Lincoln
LN1 3DY
www.bgc.ac.uk
01522 527347

Blackpool and The Fylde College
Ashfield Road
Blackpool
FY2 0HB
www.blackpool.ac.uk
01253 504346

Bolton University
Deane Road
Bolton
BL3 5AB
www.bolton.ac.uk
01204 900600

Bournemouth University
Fern Barrow
Poole
BH12 5BB
www.bournemouth.ac.uk
01202 524111

Bradford University
Richmond Road
Bradford
West Yorkshire
BD7 1DP
www.bradford.ac.uk
01274 233081

Bradford College
Great Horton Road
Bradford
West Yorkshire

BD7 1AY
www.bradfordcollege.ac.uk
01274 433333

Bridgwater College
Bath Road
Bridgwater
Somerset
TA6 4PZ
www.bridgwater.ac.uk
01278 441234

Brighton and Sussex Medical
School
University of Brighton
Ringmer House
Falmer
BN1 9PH
www.bsms.ac.uk
01273 600900

Brighton University
Mithras House
Lewes Road
Brighton
BN2 4AT
www.brighton.ac.uk
01273 644644

Bristol College
Ashley Down Centre
Ashley Down Road
Bristol
BS7 5BU
www.cityofbristol.ac.uk
0117 3125000

Bristol Filton College
Filton Avenue
Bristol
BS34 7AT
www.filton.ac.uk
0117 931 2121

Bristol University
Senate House
Tyndall Avenue
BS8 1TH
www.bristol.ac.uk
0117 928 9000

Brooklands College
Heath Road

Weybridge
KT13 8TT
www.brooklands.ac.uk
01932 797797

Brunel University
Uxbridge
Middlesex
UB8 3PH
www.brunel.ac.uk
01895 265265

Buckinghamshire Chilterns
University College
Queen Alexandra Road
High Wycombe
HP11 2JZ
www.bcuc.ac.uk
01494 605060

Buckingham University
Hunter Street
Buckingham
MK18 1EG
www.buckingham.ac.uk
01280 814080

Burton College
Lichfield Street
Burton-upon-Trent
Staffordshire
DE14 3RL
www.burton-college.ac.uk
01283 494474

Cambridge University
Fitzwilliam House
32 Trumpington Street
CB2 1QY
www.cam.ac.uk
01223 333 308

Canterbury Christ Church
University
Kent
CT1 1QU
www.canterbury.ac.uk
01227 782900

Capel Manor College
Bullsmoor Lane
Middlesex
EN1 4RQ

www.capel.ac.uk
020 8366 4442

Cardiff (University of Wales)
30-36 Newport Road
Cardiff
CF24 0DE
www.cardiff.ac.uk
029 2087 9999

Cardiff (University of Wales
Institute)
Western Avenue
Cardiff
CF5 2SG
www.uwic.ac.uk
029 2041 6070

Carmarthenshire College
Sandy Road
Llanelli
Carmarthenshire
SA15 4DN
www.colegsirgar.ac.uk
01554 748000

Carshalton College
Nightingale Road
Carshalton
Surrey
SM5 2EJ
www.carshalton.ac.uk
0208 544 4589

Castle College
Maid Marian Way
Nottingham
NG1 6AB
www.castlecollege.ac.uk
0115 884 2581

Central School of Speech and
Drama
64 Eton Avenue
London
NW3 3HY
www.cssd.ac.uk
020 7722 8183

Chester University
Parkgate Road
Chester
CH1 4BJ

www.chester.ac.uk
01244 511000

Chesterfield College
Infirmary Road
Chesterfield
S41 7NG
www.chesterfield.ac.uk
01246 500562

Chichester College
Westgate Fields
Chichester
West Sussex
PO19 1SB
www.chichester.ac.uk
01243 786321

Chichester University
College Lane
Chichester
PO19 6PE
www.chiuni.ac.uk
01243 816002

City of Bath College
Avon Street
Bath
BA1 1UP
www.citybathcoll.ac.uk
01225 312191

City College Birmingham
The Council House
Soho Road
B21 9DP
www.citycol.ac.uk
0845 050 1144

City College Coventry
Butts Centre
Butts
Coventry
CV1 3GD
www.covcollege.ac.uk
0800 616 202

City College Manchester
Manchester
M23 0GN
www.ccm.ac.uk
0800 013 0123

City of Sunderland College
Bede Centre
Durham Road
Sunderland
SR3 4AH
www.citysun.ac.uk
0191 511 6260

City University
Northampton Square
London
EC1V 0HB
www.city.ac.uk
020 7040 5060

Cleveland College of Art and
Design
Linthorpe
Middlesbrough
TS5 7RJ
www.ccad.ac.uk
01642 288888

Cliff College
Calver
Hope Valley
S32 3XG
www.cliffcollege.ac.uk
01246 584220

Colchester Institute
Sheepen Road
Colchester
Essex
CO3 3LL
www.colchester.ac.uk
01206 518777

Coleg Llandrillo Cymru
Llandudno Road
Rhos-on-Sea
Colwyn Bay
LL28 4HZ
www.llandrillo.ac.uk
01492 542338

Cornwall College
Pool
Redruth
TR15 3RD
www.cornwall.ac.uk
01209 616161

College for the Creative Arts
Falkner Road

Farnham
Surrey
GU9 7DS
www.ucreative.ac.uk
01252 892696

College of West Anglia
Tennyson Avenue
King's Lynn
PE30 2QW
www.col-westanglia.ac.uk
01553 761144

Coventry University
1 Gulson Rd
Coventry
CV1 2JH
www.coventry.ac.uk
02476 15 2222

Craven College
High Street
Skipton
North Yorkshire
BD23 1JY
www.craven-college.ac.uk
01756 791411

Croydon College
College Road
Croydon
CR9 1DX
www.croydon.ac.uk
020 8760 5948

Cumbria University
Fusehill Street
Carlisle
Cumbria
CA1 2HH
www.cumbria.ac.uk
01228 400300

Dartington College
of Arts
Totnes
Devon
TQ9 6EJ
www.dartington.ac.uk
01803 861620

Dearne Valley College
Wath-upon-Dearne
Rotherham
S63 7EW

www.dearne-coll.ac.uk
01709 513101

De Montfort University
The Gateway
Leicester
LE1 9BH
www.dmu.ac.uk
0116 255 1551

Derby University
Kedleston Road
Derby
DE22 1GB
www.derby.ac.uk
08701 202330

Dewsbury College
Halifax Road
Dewsbury
West Yorkshire
WF13 2AS
www.dewsbury.ac.uk
01924 436221

Doncaster College
Chappell Drive
Doncaster
DN1 2RF
www.don.ac.uk
01302 553610

Duchy College
Stoke Climsland
Callington
PL17 8PB
www.duchy.ac.uk
01579 372233

Dudley College of
Technology
The Broadway
Dudley
DY1 4AS
www.dudleycol.ac.uk
01384 363277

Dunstable College
Kingsway
Dunstable
Beds
LU5 4HG
www.dunstable.ac.uk
01582 477776

Durham University
University Office
Durham
DH1 3HP
www.durham.ac.uk
0191 334 2000

Ealing, Hammersmith and West
London College
Gliddon Road
London
W14 9BL
www.wlc.ac.uk
020 7565 1234

East Anglia University
Norwich
NR4 7TJ
www.uea.ac.uk
01603 456161

East Lancashire Institute of
Higher Education at Blackburn
College
Feilden Street
Blackburn
BB2 1LH
www.elihe.ac.uk
01254 292936

East Riding College
Longcroft Hall
Gallows Lane
Beverley
HU17 7DT
www.eastridingcollege.ac.uk
01482 306609

East Surrey College
Gatton Point North
Claremont Road
Redhill
RH1 2JX
www.esc.ac.uk
01737 772611

Edge Hill University
Ormskirk
Lancashire
L39 4QP
www.edgehill.ac.uk
0800 195 5063

Edinburgh College of Art
74 Lauriston Place

EH3 9DF
www.eca.ac.uk
0131 221 6027

Edinburgh University
57 George Square
Edinburgh
www.ed.ac.uk
0131 650 4360

Essex University
Wivenhoe Park
Colchester
CO4 3SQ
www.essex.ac.uk
01206 873666

European School of Economics
8/9 Grosvenor Place
Belgravia
London
SW1 7SH
www.eselondon.ac.uk
020 7245 6148

European School of
Osteopathy
Boxley House
The Street
Boxley
ME14 3DZ
www.eso.ac.uk
01622 671558

Exeter College
Victoria House
33/36 Queen Street
Exeter
EX4 3SR
www.exe-coll.ac.uk
01392 205232

Exeter University
The Queen's Drive
Exeter
EX4 4QJ
www.ex.ac.uk
01392 263035

Farnborough College of
Technology
Boundary Road
Farnborough
Hampshire
GU14 6SB

www.farn-ct.ac.uk
01252 407028

Glamorgan University
Pontypridd
Mid Glamorgan
CF37 1GY
www.glam.ac.uk
0800 716925

Glasgow University
11 Southpark Terrace
Glasgow
G12 8LG
www.gla.ac.uk
0141 330 6062

Glasgow School of Art
167 Renfrew Street
G3 6RQ
www.gsa.ac.uk
0141 353 4512

Gloucestershire College of Arts
and Technology
Brunswick Road
Gloucester
GL1 1HU
www.gloscat.ac.uk
01452 532000

Gloucestershire University
St Paul's Road
Cheltenham
GL50 4BS
www.glos.ac.uk
01242 532825

Goldsmiths College
University of London
Lewisham Way
New Cross
London
SE14 6NW
www.goldsmiths.ac.uk
020 7919 7766

Great Yarmouth College
Southtown
Great Yarmouth
Norfolk
NR31 0ED
www.gyc.ac.uk
01493 419293

Greenwich University
Old Royal Naval College
Park Row
SE10 9LS
www.gre.ac.uk
0800 005 006

Greenwich School of
Management
Meridian House
Royal Hill
Greenwich
SE10 8RD
www.greenwich-college.ac.uk
020 8516 7800

Grimsby Institute of Further and
Higher Education
Nuns Corner
Grimsby
NE Lincolnshire
DN34 5BQ
www.grimsby.ac.uk
0800 328 3631

Guildford College of Further
and Higher Education
Stoke Park
Guildford
Surrey
GU1 1EZ
www.guildford.ac.uk
01483 448500

Halton College
Kingsway
Widnes
Cheshire
WA8 7QQ
www.haltoncollege.ac.uk
0151 257 2020

Harper Adams University
College
Newport
Shropshire
TF10 8NB
www.harper-adams.ac.uk
01952 820280

Havering College of Further
and Higher Education
Ardleigh Green Road
Hornchurch
Essex

RM11 2LL
www.havering-college.ac.uk
01708 462801

Herefordshire College of Art
and Design
Folly Lane
Hereford HR1 1LT
www.hereford-art-col.ac.uk
01432 262126

Heriot-Watt University
Edinburgh
EH14 4AS
www.hw.ac.uk
0131 451 3376

Hertford Regional College
Scott's Road
Ware
Hertfordshire
SG12 9JF
www.hertreg.ac.uk
01992 411400

Heythrop College
University of London
Kensington Square
London
W8 5HQ
www.heythrop.ac.uk
020 7795 6600

Highbury College
Dovercourt Road
Cosham
Portsmouth
PO6 2SA
www.highbury.ac.uk
023 9231 3373

Holborn College
Woolwich Road
London
SE7 8LN
www.holborncollege.ac.uk
020 8317 6000

Hopwood Hall College
St Mary's Gate
Rochdale
Lancs
OL12 6RY
www.hopwood.ac.uk
01706 345346

Huddersfield Technical College
New North Road
Huddersfield
West Yorkshire
HD1 5NN
www.huddcoll.ac.uk
01484 536521

Huddersfield University
Queensgate
Huddersfield
HD1 3DH
www.hud.ac.uk
01484 422288

Hull College
Queen's Gardens
Hull
HU1 3DG
www.hull-college.ac.uk
01482 329943

Hull University
Cottingham Road
Hull
HU6 7RX
www.hull.ac.uk
01482 466100

Hull York Medical School
University of York
YO10 5DD
www.hyms.ac.uk
0870 120 2323

Imperial College London
University of London
SW7 2AZ
www.imperial.ac.uk
020 7594 8001

Islamic College for Advanced
Studies
133 High Road
Willesden
NW10 2SW
www.islamic-college.ac.uk
020 8451 9993

Keele University
Staffs
ST5 5BG
www.keele.ac.uk
01782 584005

Kensington College of Business
Wesley House
4 Wild Court
Holborn
WC2B 4AU
www.kensingtoncoll.ac.uk
020 7404 6330

Kent University
University of Kent
CT2 7NZ
www.kent.ac.uk
01227 827272

King's College London
University of London
Strand
London
WC2R 2LS
www.kcl.ac.uk
020 7836 5454

Kingston University
Cooper House
40-46 Surbiton Road
KT1 2HX
www.kingston.ac.uk
020 8547 7053

Lakes College
Hallwood Road
Lillyhall
Workington
West Cumbria
CA14 4JN
www.lakescollegewestcumbria
.ac.uk
01946 839300

Lampeter (University of Wales)
University of Wales
Lampeter
SA48 7ED
www.lamp.ac.uk
01570 422351

Lancaster University
Lancaster
Lancashire
LA1 4YW
www.lancs.ac.uk
01524 65201

Leeds College of Art & Design
Blenheim Walk

Leeds
LS2 9AQ
www.leeds-art.ac.uk
0113 202 8000

Leeds College of Music
3 Quarry Hill
Leeds
West Yorkshire
LS2 7PD
www.lcm.ac.uk
0113 222 3416

Leeds Metropolitan University
Civic Quarter
Leeds
LS1 3HE
www.leedsmet.ac.uk
0113 283 3113

Leicester College
Aylestone Road
Leicester
LE2 7LW
www.lec.ac.uk
0116 224 2240

Leeds Park Lane College
Park Lane
Leeds
LS3 1AA
www.parklanecoll.ac.uk
0113 216 2406

Leo Baeck College
80 East End Road
London
N3 2SY
www.lbc.ac.uk
020 8349 5605

Leeds Thomas Danby
College
Roundhay Road
Leeds
West Yorkshire
LS7 3BG
www.thomasdanby.ac.uk
0113 249 4912

Leeds Trinity & All Saints
Brownberrie Lane
Horsforth
Leeds
LS18 5HD

www.leedstrinity.ac.uk
0113 283 7123

Lincoln College
Monks Road
Lincoln
LN2 5HQ
www.lincolncollege.ac.uk
01522 876000

Lincoln University
Brayford Pool
LN6 7TS
www.lincoln.ac.uk
01522 886097

Leeds University
Leeds
LS2 9JT
www.leeds.ac.uk
0113 343 3999

Liverpool Hope University
Hope Park
Liverpool
L16 9JD
www.hope.ac.uk
0151 291 3295

Liverpool Institute for
Performing Arts
Mount Street
Liverpool
L1 9HF
www.lipa.ac.uk
0151 330 3000

Liverpool John Moores
University
Roscoe Court
4 Rodney Street
Liverpool
L1 2TZ
www.ljmu.ac.uk
0151 231 5090

Liverpool University
The Foundation Building
Brownlow Hill
L69 7ZX
www.liv.ac.uk
0151 794 2000

London Metropolitan
University

166-220 Holloway Road
London
N7 8DB
www.londonmet.ac.uk
020 7133 4200

London School of Commerce
Chaucer House
White Hart Yard
London
SE1 1NX
www.lsclondon.co.uk
020 7357 0077

London School of Economics
and Political Science
University of London
Houghton Street
London
WC2A 2AE
www.lse.ac.uk
020 7955 7125/7769

London South Bank University
103 Borough Road
London
SE1 0AA
www.lsbu.ac.uk
020 7815 7815

Loughborough College
Radmoor Road
Loughborough
LE11 3BT
www.loucoll.ac.uk
0845 166 2950

Loughborough University
Loughborough
Leicestershire
LE11 3TU
www.lboro.ac.uk
01509 263171

Lowestoft College
St Peter's Street
Lowestoft
Suffolk
NR32 2NB
www.lowestoft.ac.uk
01502 583521

Manchester College of Arts and
Technology

Ashton Old Road
Openshaw
M11 2WH
www.mancat.ac.uk
0800 068 8585

Manchester Metropolitan
University
All Saints Buidling
All Saints
M15 6BH
www.mmu.ac.uk
0161 247 2000

Manchester University
Oxford Road
Manchester
M13 9PL
www.manchester.ac.uk
0161 275 2077

Marjon
University College of St Mark &
St John
Derriford Road
PL6 8BH
www.marjon.ac.uk
01752 636890

Matthew Boulton College of
Further and Higher Education
Jennens Road
Birmingham
B4 7PS
www.mbc.ac.uk
0121 446 4545

Medway School of Pharmacy
PO Box 32498
London
SE18 6WD
www.gre.ac.uk
0800 005 006

Mid-Cheshire College
Northwich
Cheshire
CW8 1LJ
www.midchesh.ac.uk
01606 74444

Middlesex University
North London Business Park
Oakleigh Road South

London
N11 1QS
www.mdx.ac.uk
020 8411 5555

Myerscough College
Myerscough Hall
Bilsborrow
PR3 0RY
www.myerscough.ac.uk
01995 642222

Napier University
10 Colinton Road
Edinburgh
EH10 5DT
www.napier.ac.uk
08452 606040

New College Durham
Framwellgate Moor Centre
Durham
DH1 5ES
www.newdur.ac.uk
0191 375 4210/4211

New College Nottingham
Adams Building
Stoney Street
The Lace Market
NG1 1NG
www.ncn.ac.uk
0115 910 0100

New College Stamford
Drift Road
Stamford
Lincolnshire
PE9 1XA
www.stamford.ac.uk
01780 484300

Newcastle College
Armstrong Building
Scotswood Road
NE4 7SA
www.newcastlecollege.
co.uk
0191 200 4000

Newcastle University
6 Kensington Terrace
Newcastle upon Tyne
NE1 7RU

www.ncl.ac.uk
0191 222 5594

Newman College of Higher
Education
Genners Lane
Bartley Green
Birmingham
B32 3NT
www.newman.ac.uk
0121 476 1181

Newport (University of Wales)
Newport
NP18 3YH
www.newport.ac.uk
01633 432030

Northbrook College Sussex
Littlehampton Road
Goring by Sea
Worthing
BN12 6NU
www.northbrook.ac.uk
0800 183 6060

Northumberland College
College Road
Ashington
Northumberland
NE63 9RG
www.northland.ac.uk
01670 841200

Northumbria University
Trinity Building
Northumberland Road
Newcastle upon Tyne
NE1 8ST
www.northumbria.ac.uk
0191 243 7420

North Warwickshire and
Hinckley College
Hinckley Road
Nuneaton
Warwickshire
CV11 6BH
www.nwhc.ac.uk
024 7624 3000

Norwich City College of
Further and Higher Education
Ipswich Road

Norwich
Norfolk
NR2 2LJ
www.ccn.ac.uk
01603 773136

The Norwich School of Art and
Design
Francis House
3-7 Redwell Street
Norwich
NR2 4SN
www.nsad.ac.uk
01603 610561

Nottingham Trent University
Burton Street
Nottingham
NG1 4BU
www.ntu.ac.uk
0115 941 8418

Nottingham University
E Floor, Portland Building
University of Nottingham
NG7 2RD
www.nottingham.ac.uk
0115 951 5151

Oxford & Cherwell Valley
College
Broughton Road
Banbury
OX16 9QA
www.oxford-cherwell.ac.uk
01865 551691

Oxford Brookes University
Gipsy Lane
Oxford
OX3 0BP
www.brookes.ac.uk
01865 483040

Oxford University
Wellington Square
Oxford
OX1 2JD
www.ox.ac.uk
01865 288000

Paisley University
Paisley
Renfrewshire

Scotland
PA1 2BE
www.paisley.ac.uk
0141 848 3727

Pembrokeshire College
Haverfordwest
Pembrokeshire
SA61 1SZ
www.pembrokeshire.ac.uk
0800 716236

People's College
Maid Marian Way
Nottingham
NG1 6AB
www.peoples.ac.uk
0115 912 8582/8581

Peterborough Regional College
Park Crescent
Peterborough
PE1 4DZ
www.peterborough.ac.uk
01733 767366

Plymouth College of Art and
Design
Tavistock Place
Plymouth
PL4 8AT
www.pcad.ac.uk
01752 203434

Plymouth University
Drake Circus
Plymouth
PL4 8AA
www.plymouth.ac.uk
01752 232137

Portsmouth University
University House
Winston Churchill Avenue
PO1 2UP
www.port.ac.uk
023 9284 8484

Queen Margaret University
Clerwood Terrace
Edinburgh
EH12 8TS
www.qmuc.ac.uk
0131 317 3247

Queen Mary
University of London
Mile End Road
London
E1 4NS
www.qmul.ac.uk
020 7882 5555

Queen's University
University Road
Belfast
BT7 1NN
www.qub.ac.uk
028 9097 5081

Ravensbourne College of Design
and Communication
Walden Road
Chislehurst
Kent
BR7 5SN
www.rave.ac.uk
020 8289 4900

Reading University
Reading
RG6 6AH
www.reading.ac.uk
0118 987 5123

Regents Business School
London
Inner Circle
Regent's Park
London
NW1 4NS
www.rbslondon.ac.uk
020 7477 2992

Riverside College Halton
Kingsway
Widnes
Cheshire
WA8 7QQ
www.riversidecollege.ac.uk
0151 257 2020

Robert Gordon University
Schoolhill
Aberdeen
Scotland
AB10 1FR
www.rgu.ac.uk
01224 26 27 28

Roehampton University
Erasmus House
Roehampton Lane
London
SW15 5PU
www.roehampton.ac.uk
020 8392 3232

Rose Bruford College
Lamorbey Park
Burnt Oak Lane
Sidcup
DA15 9DF
www.bruford.ac.uk
020 8300 3024

Rotherham College of Arts and
Technology
Eastwood Lane
Rotherham
South Yorkshire
S65 1EG
www.rotherham.ac.uk
08080 722777

Royal Agricultural College
Cirencester
Glos
GL7 6JS
www.rac.ac.uk
01285 889912

Royal Holloway, University of
London
Egham
Surrey
TW20 0EX
www.rhul.c.uk
01784 434455

Royal Veterinary College
University of London
Royal College Street
London
NW1 0TU
www.rvc.ac.uk
020 7468 5149

Royal Welsh College of Music and
Drama
Castle Grounds
Cathays Park
Cardiff
CF10 3ER

www.rwcmd.ac.uk
029 2034 2854

Salford University
Salford
M5 4WT
www.salford.ac.uk
0161 295 4545

Salisbury College
Southampton Road
Salisbury
Wiltshire
SP1 2LW
www.salisbury.ac.uk
01722 344344

School of Oriental and
African Studies
University of London
Russell Square
London
WC1H 0XG
www.soas.ac.uk
020 7074 5106

The School of Pharmacy
University of London
29-39 Brunswick Square
London
WC1N 1AX
www.ulsop.ac.uk
020 7753 5831

Scottish Agricultural
College
Ayr
KA6 5HW
www.sac.ac.uk
0800 269453

St George's
University of London
Cranmer Terrace
London
SW17 0RE
www.sgul.ac.uk
020 8725 5201

St Helens College
Brook Street
St Helens
Merseyside
WA10 1PZ

www.sthelens.ac.uk
01744 733766

St Martin's College
Bowerham Road
Lancaster
Lancashire
LA1 3JD
www.ucsm.ac.uk
01524 384444

St Mary's College
Waldegrave Road
Strawberry Hill
Middlesex
TW1 4SX
www.smuc.ac.uk
020 8240 4029

Sheffield College
HE Unit
PO Box 730
Livesey Street
S6 2ET
www.sheffcol.ac.uk
0114 260 2216

Shrewsbury College of Arts and
Technology
London Road
Shrewsbury
SY2 6PR
www.shrewsbury.ac.uk
01743 342342

Sheffield University
9 Northumberland Road
Sheffield
S10 2TT
www.sheffield.ac.uk
0114 222 2000

Solihull College
Blossomfield Road
Solihull
West Midlands
B91 1SB
www.solihull.ac.uk
0121 678 7006

Somerset College of Arts and
Technology
Wellington Road
Taunton

Somerset
TA1 5AX
www.somerset.ac.uk
01823 366331

South Birmingham College
Cole Bank Road
Hall Green
B28 8ES
www.sbc.ac.uk
0121 694 5030

South Devon College
Vantage Point
Long Road
Paignton
TQ4 7JE
www.southdevon.ac.uk
08000 380123

Southampton Solent University
East Park Terrace
Southampton
Hampshire
SO14 0RT
www.solent.ac.uk
023 8031 9039

Southampton University
Highfield
Southampton
SO17 1BJ
www.soton.ac.uk
023 8059 5000

Sparsholt College Hampshire
Sparsholt
Winchester
Hampshire
SO21 2NF
www.sparsholt.ac.uk
01962 776441

South Downs College
College Road
Waterlooville
Hampshire
PO7 8AA
www.southdowns.ac.uk
023 9279 7979

South East Essex College
Luker Road
Southend-on-Sea

Essex
SS1 1ND
www.southend.ac.uk
01702 220500

South Nottingham College
West Bridgford Centre
Greythorn Drive
West Bridgford
NG2 7GA
www.snc.ac.uk
0115 914 6400

South Trafford College
Manchester Road
West Timperley
Altrincham
WA14 5PQ
www.stcoll.ac.uk
0161 952 4600

South Tyneside College
St George's Avenue
South Shields
Tyne & Wear
NE34 6ET
www.stc.ac.uk
0191 427 3500

Southport College
Mornington Road
Southport
Merseyside
PR9 0TT
www.southport-college.ac.uk
0845 00 66 236

Staffordshire University
College Road
Stoke on Trent
ST4 2DE
www.staffs.ac.uk
01782 292753

Southwark College
Waterloo Centre
The Cut
SE1 8LE
www.southwark.ac.uk
020 7815 1541

Stephenson College Coalville
Bridge Road
Coalville

Leicestershire
LE67 3PW
www.stephensoncoll.ac.uk
01530 836136

Stratford upon Avon College
The Willows North
Stratford upon Avon
Warwickshire
CV37 9QR
www.stratford.ac.uk
01789 266245 x3137

Stirling University
Stirling
FK9 4LA
www.stir.ac.uk
01786 467044

Stockport College
Wellington Road South
Stockport
SK1 3UQ
www.stockport.ac.uk
0161 958 3105

Stourbridge College
Longlands Centre
Brook Street
Stourbridge
DY8 3XB
www.stourbridge.ac.uk
01384 344600

Stranmillis University
College
Stranmillis Road
Belfast
BT9 5DY
www.stran.ac.uk
028 9038 1271

Strathclyde University
Glasgow
G1 1XQ
www.strath.ac.uk
0141 552 4400

Sutton Coldfield College
Lichfield Road
Sutton Coldfield
West Midlands
B74 2NW
www.sutcol.ac.uk
0121 362 1176

Swansea College
Tycoch Road
Tycoch
Swansea
SA2 9EB
www.swancoll.ac.uk
0800 174 084

Swansea Institute of Higher
Education
Swansea
SA1 6ED
www.sihe.ac.uk
01792 481000

Swansea (University of Wales)
Singleton Park
Swansea
SA2 8PP
www.swansea.ac.uk
01792 295111

Swindon College
Regent Circus
Swindon
Wiltshire
SN1 1PT
www.swindon-college.ac.uk
01793 498308

Tameside College
Ashton Centre
Beaufort Road
Ashton-under-Lyne
OL6 6NX
www.tameside.ac.uk
0161 908 6789

Teesside University
Middlesbrough
TS1 3BA
www.tees.ac.uk
01642 218121

Thames Valley University
St Mary's Road
Ealing
London
W5 5RF
www.tvu.ac.uk
0800 036 8888

Trinity College Carmarthen
College Road
Carmarthen

SA31 3EP
www.trinity-cm.ac.uk
01267 676767

Truro College
College Road
Truro
TR1 3XX
www.trurocollege.ac.uk
01872 267061

Tyne Metropolitan College
Embleton Avenue
Wallsend
Tyne and Wear
NE28 9NJ
www.tynemet.ac.uk
0191 229 5000

Ulster University
Coleraine
Co. Londonderry
Northern Ireland
BT52 1SA
www.ulster.ac.uk
028 7032 4221

University of the Arts London
65 Davies Street
London
W1K 5DA
www.arts.ac.uk
020 7514 6000

University College for the
Creative Arts
(formerly Kent Institute of Art
and Design)
Fort Pitt
Rochester
ME1 1DZ
www.ucreative.ac.uk
01634 888773

University College London
University of London
Gower Street
London
WC1E 6BT
www.ucl.ac.uk
020 7679 3000

University of Central England
Perry Barr
Birmingham

B42 2SU
www.uce.ac.uk
0121 331 5595

University of Central
Lancashire
Preston
Lancs
PR1 2HE
www.uclan.ac.uk
01772 201201

University of Dundee
Dundee
DD1 4HN
www.dundee.ac.uk
01382 384160

University College
Falmouth
Woodlane
Falmouth
Cornwall
TR11 4RH
www.falmouth.ac.uk
01326 211077

University of East
London
4-6 University Way
E16 2RD
www.uel.ac.uk
020 8223 2835

University of Hertfordshire
College Lane
Hatfield
AL10 9AB
www.herts.ac.uk
01707 284800

University of Leicester
University Road
Leicester
LE1 7RH
www.le.ac.uk
0116 252 5281

University of St Andrews
St Katherine's West, The
Scores
St Andrews
KY16 9AX
www.st-and.ac.uk
01334 462150

University of the West of
England, Bristol
Coldharbour Lane
Bristol
BS16 1QY
www.uwe.ac.uk
0117 328 3333

Uxbridge College
Park Road
Uxbridge
Middlesex
UB8 1NQ
www.uxbridgecollege.ac.uk
01895 853333

Wakefield College
Margaret Street
Wakefield
WF1 2DH
www.wakefield.ac.uk
01924 789111

Walsall College
St Paul's Street
Walsall
WS1 1XN
www.walcat.ac.uk
01922 657000

Warrington Collegiate
Winwick Road
Warrington
WA2 8QA
www.warrington.ac.uk
01925 494494

Warwick University
University of Warwick
Coventry
CV4 8UW
www.warwick.ac.uk
024 7652 3723

Warwickshire College
Warwick New Road
Leamington Spa
Warwickshire
CV32 5JE
www.warkscol.ac.uk
01926 318000

Welsh College of Horticulture
Holywell Road
Northop

Mold
CH7 6AA
www.wcoh.ac.uk
01352 841000

West Cheshire College
Eaton Road
Handbridge
Chester
CH4 7ER
www.west-cheshire.ac.uk
01244 670600

West Herts College
Hempstead Road
Watford
Herts
WD17 3EZ
www.westherts.ac.uk
01923 812345

University of Westminster
35 Marylebone Road
London
NW1 5LS
www.wmin.ac.uk
020 7911 5000

West Suffolk College
Out Risbygate
Bury St Edmunds
Suffolk
IP33 3RL
www.westsuffolk.ac.uk
01284 716333

West Thames College
London Road
Isleworth
Middlesex
TW7 4HS
www.west-thames.ac.uk
020 8326 2020

Westminster Kingsway
College
Vincent Square Centre
Vincent Square
London
SW1P 2PD
www.westking.ac.uk
020 7556 8001

Wigan and Leigh College
Parsons Walk

Wigan
WN1 1RS
www.wigan-leigh.ac.uk
01942 761605

Wimbledon School of Art
Merton Hall Road
London
SW19 3QA
www.wimbledon.ac.uk
020 8408 5000

Wirral Metropolitan College
Europa Boulevard
Birkenhead, Wirral
CH41 4NT
www.wmc.ac.uk
0151 551 7777

Wiltshire College
Cocklebury Road
Chippenham
Wiltshire
SN15 3QD
www.wiltscoll.ac.uk
01249 464644

Winchester University
Winchester
Hampshire

SO22 4NR
www.winchester.ac.uk
01962 827234

Worcester College of
Technology
Deansway
Worcester
WR1 2JF
www.wortech.ac.uk
01905 725555

Wolverhampton University
Compton Road West
Wolverhampton
WV3 9DX
www.wlv.ac.uk
01902 321000

Worcester University
Henwick Grove
Worcester
WR2 6AJ
www.worcester.ac.uk
01905 855111

Writtle College
Chelmsford
Essex
CM1 3RR

www.writtle.ac.uk
01245 424200

York College
Tadcaster Road
York
YO24 1UA
www.yorkcollege.ac.uk
01904 770400

York St John University
Lord Mayor's Walk
York
YO31 7EX
www.yorksj.ac.uk
01904 716598

York University
University of York
Heslington
YO10 5DD
www.york.ac.uk
01904 433533

Index